Wild Feasts

Then an old man, a keeper of an inn, said, Speak to us of Eating and Drinking.

And he said:

Would that you could live on the fragrance of the earth, and like an air plant be sustained by the light.

But since you must kill to eat, and rob the newly born of its mother's milk to quench your thirst, let it then be an act of worship.

And let your board stand an altar on which the pure and the innocent of forest and plain are sacrificed for that which is purer and still more innocent in man.

When you kill a beast say to him in your heart,

"By the same power that slays you, I too am slain; and I too shall be consumed.

For the law that delivered you into my hand shall deliver me into a mightier hand.

Your blood and my blood is naught but the sap that feeds the tree of heaven."

—*From* The Prophet
by Kahlil Gibran

*To our fish and wildlife, the lands and waters
they inhabit, and to those conservationists
who revere and sustain them.*

DUCKS UNLIMITED, INC.

The mission of Ducks Unlimited is to fulfill the annual life
cycle needs of North American waterfowl by protecting,
enhancing, restoring, and managing important wetlands
and associated uplands. Since its inception in 1937, DU
has raised more than $1 billion, which has contributed to
the conservation of over eight million acres of prime
wildlife habitat in all fifty states, each of the Canadian
provinces and in key areas of Mexico. In the U.S. alone,
DU has helped to conserve over 1 million acres of waterfowl habitat. Some 600 species of wildlife live and flour-
ish on DU projects, including many threatened or endan-
gered species.

Wild Feasts

DUCKS UNLIMITED GAME AND FISH COOKBOOK

Edited and Designed by Diane Jolie

Ducks Unlimited, Inc.
Memphis, Tennessee
1997

Editor and Book Designer: Diane Jolie
Introduction and Chapter Commentary: Billy Joe Cross
Recipes Editor: Katherine Lee
Published by Ducks Unlimited, Inc.
Gene M. Henry, President
John E. Walker, Chairman of the Board
Matthew B. Connolly, Jr., Executive Vice President
Chris Dorsey, Group Manager of Publishing and Communications

ISBN 1-57223-130-0

Library of Congress Cataloging-in-Publication Data

Wild Feasts: Ducks Unlimited game and fish cookbook /
edited and designed by Diane Jolie.
    p.   cm.
Includes index.
ISBN 1-57223-130-0
1. Cookery (Game). 2. Cookery (Fish). I. Jolie, Diane,
1963- . II. Ducks Unlimited.
TX751.W4696   1997   97-33286
641.6′91—dc21   CIP

Published August 1997
Printed in the U.S.A. by
The Wimmer Companies

Contents

Introduction

As every hunter knows, *cooking* wild game is as exciting and gratifying as *hunting* it. After a day spent outdoors, appetites are strong, and nothing can erase the elemental satisfaction found in bringing to table steaming platters of meat harvested by one's own hand. The tantalizing aroma is made all the more enticing by the memories of the hunt.

Because hunters are also innately conservationists, we are always in pursuit of new and ever more delectable ways of preparing the day's take. The recipes in this book easily guide us in those ventures by offering a veritable smorgasbord, from appetizers and soups to desserts and beverages, with plenty of attention to savory main courses. We asked the readers of *Ducks Unlimited* magazine to contribute their favorite recipes, and they responded with the same generous outpouring that has made Ducks Unlimited the largest wetlands and waterfowl conservation organization in the world. Judging from the recipes we received, I think it is safe to say that DU readers are the best *cooks* in the world. You'll find dishes to please the most discriminating of tastes and enough variety to pique your interest throughout the seasons. This is the kind of authentic, down-home food that satisfies the taste buds and soothes the soul.

As you turn the pages of this book, I predict that you will begin to notice a hollow feeling in the pit of your stomach and you will suddenly realize how hungry you are. Just browsing through the recipes will make you want to go straight to your freezer and take out that carefully wrapped package you've been saving for just the "right" recipe. Wild game is a precious commodity that deserves the utmost care in preparation and the perfect blend of seasonings. These recipes will guide you, in an easy-to-read format, from start to finish. The recipes come from *Ducks Unlimited* readers, but the accolades from friends and loved ones will be yours. Enjoy.

—*Billy Joe Cross*

Foreword

A Measure of Heritage

No outdoor calling can parallel the traditions and grandeur of North American wildfowling, a pursuit rooted in legend and lore. The waterfowl hunter's passion for ducks, geese, and other wildlife, and the places these creatures inhabit, transcends geographical affinity, occupational differences, personal politics, and so-called generation gaps.

And it is the wildfowler and other hunters and anglers, more than any other single group of citizens, who have championed the cause of wildlife conservation. Historically, as they do today, hunters and anglers have assumed the bulk of the financial responsibilities of conserving wildlife—through license and stamp fees, special excise taxes, and support of private-sector conservation organizations like Ducks Unlimited. They understand that they are doing the right thing, what *must* be done, and the duration and depth of their mutual commitment to our natural resources will tell the ultimate conservation story—and perpetuate the sounds of whistling wings.

There are many rewards for those who spend time afield. Rewards that transpire while sharing a cramped duck blind or goose pit with family and friends. Or perhaps while sitting in wait on a well-placed deer stand or casting a tight loop over a sparkling trout stream. Or while watching a bird dog close in on an elusive pheasant, quail, or grouse. Special moments all. Moments that make memories. These experiences are the hunter's and angler's ultimate payback.

Preparing fish and game for the table is another reward. Wild game cookery has come a long way since our forefathers began roasting teal and trout on sticks propped over campfires. Today, cooking nature's bounty has evolved into an art form, reflecting the varied backgrounds and personal tastes of sportsmen and women across the continent. Duck camps have their special recipes too, time-honored favorites that every year seem to improve with age. And so do hunting and fishing families, who pass down fish and game preparation skills from generation to generation.

In the pages that follow, those sportsmen and women, duck camp chefs, and families gladly invite you to share in their bounty of wild feasts, and to regale in a measure of the proud legacy of North American hunters and anglers.

—Matthew B. Connolly, Jr.
Executive Vice President, Ducks Unlimited

Starters and Sides

The best meals begin with flavorful tidbits that excite the palate, preparing it for the "main attraction," the entree. You'll find that the recipes in this section do both, as well as provide tempting side dishes and breads to complement the main course. Simple enough for quiet family dinners and elegant enough for company, these are great additions to any meal.

—*Billy Joe Cross*

Sharptail Grouse Pâté

Pâté freezes well, so make it ahead of time when planning for guests. Allow it to defrost completely before serving.

1½ pounds grouse breasts
1 cup water
1½ cups butter or margarine
6 tablespoons minced onion
1½ teaspoons salt

½ teaspoon nutmeg
¼ teaspoon ground cloves
¼ teaspoon cayenne pepper
2 teaspoons dry mustard

Simmer grouse in 1 cup water for 1 to 1½ hours or until tender. Process butter and next 6 ingredients in a food processor or blender. Remove meat from bone, and add to mixture in the food processor; blend until smooth. Serve with crackers.

—Gordon Arnold
Regina, Saskatchewan

Waterfowl Pâté

**1 pound waterfowl livers
  (about 2 cups)**
1 cup water
3 teaspoons Lawry's salt

1 garlic clove
½ small onion
2 (8-ounce) packages cream cheese

Bring first 4 ingredients to a boil; boil until livers are done, and let cool in broth. Puree livers and onion. Add enough broth to make a paste. Boil the remaining broth until reduced to about ¼ cup. Stir the broth and cream cheese into the liver mixture. Chill. Serve with crackers or toasted bread.

- *Add ½ cup red wine to the broth before reducing.*
- *Add 3 dried mushrooms to livers when boiling.*
- *Add 1 tablespoon coarsely cracked black pepper or 1 tablespoon hot sauce or hot peppers.*

*—Ceil Schaeffer
Sheboygan, Wisconsin*

If waterfowl is not available, substitute chicken livers. This is a great recipe to vary and stylize to your fancy, and it also freezes well.

Venison Meatballs

1 pound ground venison
1 egg
1 medium onion, finely chopped
1 tablespoon garlic salt
Black pepper to taste

3 tablespoons vegetable oil
1 cup ketchup
½ cup vinegar
1 cup brown sugar
Hot sauce to taste (optional)

Since this appetizer needs to chill overnight, plan ahead. Ground elk or other ground meat can be substituted for venison.

Combine first 5 ingredients in a large bowl, stirring well. Roll mixture into ¾- to 1-inch balls. Chill overnight. Brown meatballs in hot oil in a large skillet. Cook ketchup and next 3 ingredients in a separate skillet over medium heat until sugar melts. Combine meatballs and sauce in a slow cooker, and cook on high about 4 hours.

—James Thornton, Sr.
Creal Springs, Illinois

16

Duck Breast Teriyaki Appetizer

2 boneless wild duck breast halves,
    cut into 1-inch cubes
½ cup Teriyaki sauce
1 tablespoon soy sauce

1 tablespoon peanut oil
1 teaspoon minced fresh ginger
8 to 10 bacon slices, cut in half
16 to 20 pineapple chunks

Combine first 5 ingredients in a small bowl. Marinate for 1 hour. Place 1 duck cube and 1 pineapple chunk on a piece of bacon. Roll up, and secure with a wooden pick. Cook at 550° for 10 minutes or until bacon is crisp.

—*Jim Waldman*
Houston, Texas

These tasty treats go fast. If friends will be dropping by, you might want to double or triple the recipe.

Pickled Pike

1 quart northern pike
½ cup salt
White vinegar
Sliced onion

3 tablespoons pickling spices
2 cups white wine vinegar
1 cup sugar

If you like pickled herring, you'll love this recipe. Pike's pure white flesh is delicious and this recipe eliminates the hassles of the pike's prevalent "Y" bones.

Fillet fish, removing skin, large backbone, and rib cage. Small forked bones can be left in. Cut fillets into 2-inch square pieces. Layer fish in a glass bowl, and salt each layer. Cover fish with white vinegar; cover bowl, and chill for 5 days, stirring each day. Rinse fish in cold water; let stand in cold water for 1 hour. Layer fish and onion in 1-quart jars. Add pickling spices. Combine white wine vinegar and sugar, and pour over fish. Cover jars, but do not seal; chill. Let marinate 4 or 5 days. Serve with saltines or round buttery crackers. Store in the refrigerator for months.

—*Jim "Polski" Pawlowski*
Cudahy, Wisconsin

Morgan Hill Goose Nuggets

2 goose breasts, cut into
   1-inch squares
4 eggs
2 to 3 garlic cloves, minced
¼ cup parsley, minced

1 cup Italian-style breadcrumbs
Salt and pepper to taste
¼ cup olive oil
1 to 2 cups white wine

Combine first 4 ingredients, and let marinate 4 to 8 hours. Dredge goose in bread-crumbs, and salt and pepper to taste. Brown in hot oil until golden on all sides. Place in a roasting pan. Pour wine over top. Bake at 400° for 5 to 10 minutes. Serve hot.

—Bob Henke
Morgan Hill, California

For a crisp, delicious treat, you can't beat goose nuggets. You can also substitute duck for goose. Double the breast count when using small ducks, such as teal.

Grilled Goose Appetizer

2 boneless goose breasts
1 (12.7-ounce) bottle hickory smoke-
flavor Allegro Marinade

1 (6-ounce) bottle hot sauce
1 pound bacon slices

This simple but delectable recipe may also be used to prepare squirrel, pheasant, deer tender-loin, or even dove. Before skewering the meat, soak the picks in hot water to prevent scorching the wood.

Soak goose breasts in salt water to cover for at least 2 hours. Drain, rinse, and cut into 1-inch cubes. Combine goose cubes, marinade, and hot sauce; chill 4 hours or overnight. Cut each bacon slice in half lengthwise and then in half crosswise. Wrap each goose cube with a piece of bacon, and secure with a wooden pick. Grill goose appetizers over medium heat (300° to 350°) until done.

—*Danny and Angie Bush*
Carbondale, Illinois

Golden Brown Duck Wraps

**Teal breast fillets or duck breasts cut
    into 2- x 3-inch pieces**
Jalapeño peppers, halved and seeded
Onion, sliced into 1- x 2-inch pieces
Bacon slices

Egg
Milk
Pancake mix
Vegetable oil

Boil teal fillets in seasoned water to cover until done. Pat fillets dry. Place 1 jalapeño pepper half and 1 onion slice between 2 fillets. Wrap with 1 bacon slice, and secure with wooden picks. Repeat with remaining teal fillets, jalapeño, and onion. Combine egg and milk, and dredge fillets in mixture. Dredge in pancake mix. Fry fillets in hot oil until golden brown.

—*Robert Florus*
Mont Belvieu, Texas

If you don't like spicy food, soak the jalapeños in water, and refrigerate for 1 day. This will eliminate some of the heat but leave the flavor. For seasoned water, add Creole seasoning, Italian dressing, and a splash of red cooking wine to water.

DU

Grilled Jalapeño Goose Poppers

These are called poppers because they are so tasty that you want to pop them into your mouth straight from the grill. Watch out for the wooden picks!

1 goose or duck breast, cut into 1- x 3-inch strips
Italian dressing

20 jalapeño peppers, sliced lengthwise and seeded
½ pound bacon

Combine goose strips and Italian dressing to cover, and chill 2 hours. Place 1 goose strip between 2 jalapeño slices, and wrap with 1 bacon slice; secure with wooden picks. Repeat with remaining goose strips, jalapeño, and bacon. Grill over medium heat (300° to 350°) for 30 minutes, turning every 5 minutes.

—J. T. Kelso
Dalhart, Texas

Cajun Goose Strips

2 goose breast fillets
Cajun Magic Poultry Seasoning

2 to 4 tablespoons butter

Slice goose fillets across the grain into 1- x 3-inch strips, and dredge in poultry seasoning. Melt butter in a large skillet or on an aluminum foil-covered grill. Cook goose strips over medium heat for 2 minutes on each side.

—*Richard Fowler*
Danville, Kentucky

These crispy favorites make a great appetizer and can also be served for the main course. For the best flavor, cook the goose medium rare to medium.

Universal Jerky

Store jerky in a paper bag for the first few days. For long-term storage, zip-top plastic bags or airtight jars work well. Do not refrigerate. This jerky will last 1 year, or longer, and taste delicious from one hunting season to the next.

Meat for jerky (deer, beef, turkey, duck, or goose)
Seasoned salt
Sugar
Black pepper

Garlic powder (optional)
Crushed red pepper (optional)
Colgin hickory-flavored liquid smoke
Worcestershire sauce
Hot sauce (optional)

Cut meat into strips for drying. Combine dry ingredients using 3 parts seasoned salt, 3 parts sugar, 2 parts black pepper, and, if desired, a pinch of garlic powder and red pepper to taste. Layer meat in a large container, sprinkling each layer with dry seasoning mix, liquid smoke, Worcestershire sauce, and, if desired, hot sauce. Marinate in the refrigerator 24 hours or several days, turning container over occasionally. Dry marinated meat in a dehydrator or an oven set on the lowest setting with the racks lined with crumpled aluminum foil, checking and rotating trays every 8 hours. Some pieces will dry in 8 hours; others may take up to 2 days.

—*Robert Slatton*
Doyle, Tennessee

Homemade Venison Jerky

2 pounds venison, trimmed and
   sliced with the grain into ⅛- to
   ¼-inch thick strips
Vegetable oil
Ground pepper to taste
2 tablespoons Worcestershire
2 tablespoons soy sauce

2 tablespoons dried thyme
2 tablespoons dried oregano
1 tablespoon salt
2 garlic cloves, minced
3 tablespoons brown sugar
1 to 1½ cups water
½ cup whiskey, red wine, or beer

Brown venison strips in hot oil in a large skillet, turning often and sprinkling with
pepper to taste. Combine Worcestershire and next 8 ingredients in a large bowl. Add
venison, and marinate 24 hours. Remove venison from marinade, discarding
marinade; pat dry. Cook on a baking sheet at 150° (with oven door partially open)
3 to 4½ hours, turning after 1½ hours. Pepper lightly on each side.

—Ray A. Ruth
Richmond, Virginia

The key to this jerky is to not overcook it. Store the tasty treat in the freezer and enjoy it year-round.

Baked Elk Jerky

Adjust this marinade as
you see fit. If you like a
milder flavor, reduce
the red pepper and
liquid smoke. Don't
eliminate them altogether
because you need a
little kick to make good
jerky.

1 teaspoon ground red pepper
1 tablespoon salt
1 teaspoon onion powder
1 teaspoon garlic powder
½ teaspoon ground black pepper
2 tablespoons liquid smoke
1 tablespoon sugar
1 cup warm water
3 pounds elk meat, sliced into thin
strips
Freshly ground black pepper to taste

Combine first 8 ingredients, stirring until seasonings are dissolved. Combine marinade and elk strips in a 3-quart baking dish; cover and chill 16 hours. Remove meat from marinade, discarding marinade; pat dry. Add freshly ground pepper to taste. Line the bottom of the oven with foil, and hang elk strips directly from oven racks. Cook at 150° about 4 hours. Check often for dryness.

—Edith Ferrario
Central Point, Oregon

Cold Smoked Goose Jerky

1 quart water
½ cup soy sauce
½ cup Worcestershire sauce
2 tablespoons Accent
2 tablespoons salt
2 tablespoons onion powder
1 tablespoon poultry seasoning
1 tablespoon garlic powder

1 tablespoon ground black pepper
1 tablespoon ground white pepper
1 tablespoon ground red pepper
1 tablespoon chili powder
2 boneless goose breasts, sliced into
   ¼-inch-thick strips
Wood chips
Salt and black pepper to taste

Combine first 12 ingredients, stirring well. Add goose strips, and marinate overnight. Remove goose strips from marinade, discarding marinade. Place strips on baking sheets, and let dry 1½ hours before smoking. Prepare charcoal fire in smoker; let burn 15 to 20 minutes. Place wood chips on coals. Place water pan in smoker; add water to depth of fill line. Sprinkle strips lightly with salt and pepper, and place on food racks. Do not overlap. Cover with smoker lid. Cook 4 to 6 hours or until strips are flexible but not moist on the inside, turning strips occasionally and alternating rack positions. Change smoking chips about every 1½ hours.

Yield: 50 to 75 pieces of jerky.

—*Bob Meyers*
Wind Gap, Pennsylvania

This recipe also works well if the meat is dried in the oven. Just hang the goose strips from the oven racks, and cook at 200° (with the oven door partially open) about 8 hours.

Best-Ever Goose Jerky

Fill several zip-top plastic bags with this delicious jerky for your next hunting trip. Your hunting partners will greatly appreciate the savory snack.

½ cup teriyaki or soy sauce
½ cup sherry
½ cup olive oil
1 medium onion, finely sliced
3 garlic cloves, sliced
15 juniper berries, crushed

2 teaspoons ground ginger
1 teaspoon grated orange rind
3 to 4 boneless goose breasts, sliced
  into thin strips
Salt and pepper to taste

Combine first 8 ingredients in a shallow dish, stirring well. Add goose strips, and chill several days to 1 week, turning daily. Place strips on oven racks or in a dehydrator, and cook at 140° for 8 hours on each side or until desired degree of doneness. Store in zip-top plastic bags in the refrigerator. Do not freeze (the flavor of the meat will drastically change).

—*Walt Wood*
Shelbyville, Tennessee

Geesey Wild Rice Hotdish

1½ cups cooked wild rice
2 cans cream of celery soup
1 cup sliced mushrooms
1 cup chicken broth

1 to 2 cups leftover cooked and
    cubed goose and gravy
Pepper to taste
1 can French fried onions

Combine the first 6 ingredients, stirring well. Pour into a lightly greased 3-quart baking dish. Top with onions. Bake at 325° for 1 hour.

—*Chris Herzog*
Aurora, Minnesota

For a heartier side dish, add 1 cup of vegetables, such as peas or green beans. Almost any combination will add new character to this delicious dish.

Stormin' Norman's Red Beans and Rice

1 (2½-pound) bone-in ham
1 pound dried red or pinto beans
1 large onion, chopped
2 garlic bulbs, chopped

Fat rendered from 1 to 3 pounds
 bacon
1 pound long-grain rice, cooked

Many years of testing have gone into perfecting this recipe. Feeding your dog while cooking is, of course, optional.

Bone the ham. Give the bone to your retriever. Cut the ham into 2- to 3-inch cubes. Rinse and pick over the beans. Place beans in a large pot, and cover with water to a depth of 1 inch above the beans. Bring to boil over high heat; add onion and garlic. Reduce heat, and simmer. Fry bacon in a large skillet until crisp. Drain and pour the fat into the beans. Give the bacon to your retriever. Add the ham to the beans. Cover and simmer, stirring occasionally, for 2 to 3 hours or until the beans reach desired creaminess. Be careful towards the end of the cooking that the bottom of the pot doesn't burn. If it does, stop stirring, and immediately pour beans into a clean pot. Give the old pot to your retriever to clean. Spoon rice onto individual plates, and top with beans and ham. Serve with hot or mild sausage, cornbread or French bread, cooked greens, and even game or fish. Pass hot sauce, salt, and pepper at the table. If all this is done right, look out the back door and see your retriever smilin'.

—Norman Mcinnis IV
Mobile, Alabama

Doctored Baked Beans

1 teaspoon dry mustard
¾ cup brown sugar
2 (16-ounce) cans baked beans

½ cup ketchup
¼ cup onion, chopped
4 bacon slices, cooked and cut up

Combine mustard and brown sugar. Layer beans and sugar mixture in a baking dish. Top with ketchup. Add onion, stirring well. Sprinkle with bacon pieces. Bake at 325° for 3 hours.

Yields: 6 to 8 servings.

—*Julie "Bean" Harvey*
Toledo, Ohio

For a bite in your beans, omit the mustard, and substitute tangy barbecue sauce for ketchup.

31

Wild Rice-and-Bread Stuffing

*Rice and stuffing are
ideal accompaniments
to wild game. This
recipe combines two
favorites into one
delicious side dish.
You'll want to make
extra because leftovers
freeze well.*

½ cup raisins
2 to 2¼ cups chicken broth, divided
3 cups cooked wild rice
6 cups soft breadcrumbs
½ cup diced onion

2 celery stalks, diced
2 Haraldson apples, chopped
½ cup butter or margarine, melted
1 teaspoon dried sage
1 teaspoon dried thyme

Combine raisins and 1 cup chicken broth; let stand until raisins are plumped. Combine raisins, broth, rice, and breadcrumbs in a large bowl. Sauté onion and celery in a skillet until tender; add to raisin mixture. Add apple, butter, and seasonings; toss well. Add remaining 1 to 1¼ cups chicken broth as needed to moisten. Spoon dressing into a lightly greased 1½-quart casserole. Bake at 350° for 20 to 30 minutes, or microwave at HIGH 10 minutes.

Yields: 6 to 8 servings.

—*Tom and Anita Wise*
Le Sueur, Minnesota

Boy Scout Potatoes

5 bacon slices
3 pounds red potatoes, skinned
5 large carrots

2 medium onions, peeled
2 celery stalks
2 tablespoons bacon grease

Place bacon on a sheet of heavy-duty aluminum foil. Slice potatoes over bacon. Quarter carrots, onions, and celery; place on top of potato slices. Spread bacon grease over top. Wrap tightly, and grill over medium heat (350° to 400°) until foil expands. Unwrap and serve; season to taste.

Yield: 6 servings.

—*Greg Gittings*
Havre de Grace, Maryland

Campers may want to chop the vegetables before leaving home. When arriving at the campsite, simply combine the ingredients, and heat. You'll love this recipe in your own backyard too.

DU

33

"As You Like It" Hushpuppies

Hushpuppies may be varied to suit your taste. Try adding a hot chile pepper or two for a southwestern flavor.

1 cup cornmeal
⅓ cup flour
1 teaspoon salt
2 teaspoons baking powder

1 medium onion, chopped
¾ cup cold water
Vegetable oil

Combine all ingredients, and let stand 30 minutes to 1 hour. Add more water, if necessary, to reach desired consistency. Drop by teaspoonfuls into hot oil, dipping spoon into oil each time. Fry until lightly browned, turning once.

- *To make beer hushpuppies, substitute ¾ bottle room temperature beer for water. If more liquid is needed, use water. Proceed as directed.*
- *To make corn hushpuppies, add 1 small can sweet corn, drained, to batter. Proceed as directed.*

—*Terry Vos*
Burlington, Wisconsin

34

Skillet Custard Corn Bread

1½ cups cornmeal
½ cup flour
1 teaspoon baking powder
1 teaspoon salt
1 teaspoon baking soda

1 tablespoon brown sugar
2 eggs
1 cup buttermilk
2 cups milk, divided
2 tablespoons butter or margarine

Combine first 6 ingredients in a large bowl. Combine eggs, buttermilk, and 1 cup of milk in a separate bowl. Add to dry ingredients, stirring just until moistened. Melt butter in a 10-inch iron skillet, coating bottom and sides. Add batter to skillet, and pour remaining 1 cup milk in the center. Do not stir. Bake at 350° for 30 minutes. Cut into wedges, and serve with butter.

—Jock Mutschler
Rochester, New York

For those tired of dry, crumbling corn bread, try this skillet version of the old favorite. Its moist texture gives it a whole new taste.

DU

35

Mexican Cornbread

Different chile peppers may be used to vary the heat of this dish. For fiery hot cornbread, substitute habañero peppers. For milder cornbread, seed the jalapeños before chopping.

1 cup cornmeal
1 cup buttermilk
½ teaspoon salt
¾ teaspoon baking soda
1 (8-ounce) can cream corn
2 eggs

1 small onion, chopped
2 jalapeño peppers, chopped
¼ cup oil
8 ounces sharp Cheddar cheese, grated

Combine first 8 ingredients in a large bowl. Heat oil in a heavy skillet. Pour in half of batter, and sprinkle with half of cheese. Pour in remaining batter, and top with remaining cheese. Bake at 400° for 30 minutes.

— "Wild" Bill Goebel
Granger, New Mexico

Belgian Bean Potato Salad

6 to 8 new potatoes (about ¾ pound), unpeeled
1 pound green beans
2 tablespoons unsalted butter or vegetable oil
1 (5-ounce) bacon slab, cut into 1- x ¼-inch strips
¼ cup red wine vinegar
Salt to taste
2 shallots or 1 small onion, finely chopped
¼ cup minced fresh parsley
Freshly ground pepper to taste

Cook the potatoes in boiling salted water to cover about 20 minutes or until tender; drain, and allow to cool slightly. Cook the green beans in boiling salted water to cover 10 to 15 minutes or until crisp-tender. (Do not cover the pot or they will discolor.) Peel the potatoes, and cut each into 4 pieces. Combine the potato and warm green beans in a large bowl. Melt the butter or heat the oil in a medium skillet over medium heat. Add the bacon, and sauté 4 to 6 minutes or until crisp but not too brown. Pour the bacon and drippings over the potato and green beans. Add vinegar to the skillet, and cook over high heat 1 minute or until reduced by two-thirds. Pour vinegar over the vegetables, and toss to coat. Add salt to taste. Sprinkle with shallots, parsley, and freshly ground pepper to taste.

Yield: 4 servings.

—*Kathy Jensen*
Hinsdale, Illinois

You will love this delicious warm salad. The bacon-red vinaigrette also tastes great over lettuce.

DU

37

Cole Slaw with Cooked Dressing

This salad is ideal to prepare in the morning for the evening meal because it needs to be made several hours before eating.

1 small cabbage, shredded
1 small onion, diced
2 carrots, shredded
1 tablespoon celery seed

Salt to taste
¾ cup vinegar
1¼ cups sugar
¾ cup vegetable oil

Combine first 5 ingredients in a large bowl. Bring vinegar, sugar, and oil to a boil in a saucepan. Pour over cabbage mixture. Chill at least 3 hours.

—*Joe Knoblauch*
Hopkins, Minnesota

SOUPS AND SAUCES

What better way to start a meal than with a cup of hot soup, rich with vegetables or cheese, bits of meat or seafood, and seasoned just right? Actually, a whole bowl of some of the following soups will be hearty enough on their own to satisfy the hungriest hunter. Then, as gourmands often declare, "the proof is in the sauce." And who doesn't love meats that have been steeped in tangy marinades or covered in savory condiments?

—Billy Joe Cross

Groucho's Duck Soup

4 tablespoons butter or margarine
1 onion, finely chopped
4 to 5 boneless duck breasts,
    cut into 1-inch cubes
3 cups beef bouillon granules

½ tablespoon garlic powder
2 bay leaves
Salt and freshly ground pepper
    to taste
1 cup barley or barley soup mix

Melt butter in a large skillet. Add onion, and cook 3 to 4 minutes or until browned. Add duck cubes, and cook until browned, stirring constantly. Combine onion, duck, 2 cups bouillon, garlic powder, bay leaves, and salt and pepper to taste in a 2-quart baking dish. Cover and microwave at HIGH 3 minutes. Stir once, and microwave at LOW (10% power) 20 minutes. Add barley and remaining 1 cup bouillon. Cover loosely, and microwave at MEDIUM (50% power) 20 minutes. Remove bay leaves, and discard. Let stand at room temperature 5 minutes before serving.

—Jim Waldman
Houston, Texas

Serve this flavorful soup with crusty French bread. A cold beer and a classic Groucho Marx movie are both optional accompaniments.

Gadwall Noodle Soup

½ cup wild rice
2 gadwall breasts, cut into
   1-inch cubes
1 onion, chopped
1 garlic clove, minced
2 tablespoons olive oil
1 (28-ounce) can whole tomatoes
2 cups chicken bouillon granules
2 cups water
1 cup shredded cabbage

1 zucchini, sliced
2 carrots, sliced
1 tablespoon dried parsley flakes
¼ teaspoon black pepper
¼ teaspoon browning-and-seasoning
   sauce
1 teaspoon Worcestershire sauce
1 bay leaf
1 cup wide egg noodles

Soak wild rice in water to cover overnight. Cook gadwall cubes, onion, and garlic in hot oil in a large heavy skillet until gadwall is browned. Drain rice, and add to skillet. Add tomatoes and next 10 ingredients; simmer 45 minutes. Add noodles, and simmer 15 minutes. Remove and discard bay leaf.

—Nora Taylor
Burns, Oregon

While gadwall tastes great in this flavorful soup, other ducks, such as mallards, work well in its place.

Duck Soup with Endive

Endive may be found in two forms. One has divided leaves, which curl under. The other type has wide, fleshy leaves. Either may be used for this savory soup. Stir-fry the chopped endive in a skillet for 10 minutes. Leaves should be wilted before placing them in the Dutch oven.

1 pound endive, chopped and cooked
1 large or 2 small ducks, cut into
    small pieces
8 cups water
2 celery stalks with leaves, chopped
1 large carrot, sliced
1 large onion, diced
1 teaspoon salt
6 chicken bouillon cubes
1 cup water (optional)

Simmer first 8 ingredients in a large Dutch oven 2 to 3 hours. Add 1 cup water, if desired, to reach desired thickness. Top each serving with seasoned croutons.

—Debbie Bellino
New Middletown, Ohio

42

Duck Soup Olé

4 mallard, black, or pintail ducks,
  cleaned and rinsed
½ onion
1 carrot, sliced into large pieces
3 or 4 leafy celery tops
1 garlic clove, minced or ½ teaspoon
  garlic powder
4 bay leaves (optional)
4 or 5 whole allspice (optional)

6 to 8 carrots, sliced diagonally
1 onion, cut in half lengthwise
6 to 8 celery stalks, sliced diagonally
1½ to 2 cups salsa
1 (12-ounce) can tomato paste
Salt to taste
5 to 6 cups wide egg noodles, cooked
1 tablespoon butter or margarine

Combine first 5 ingredients and, if desired, bay leaves and allspice in a large stockpot. Bring close to a boil. Do not boil. Reduce heat, cover, and simmer until meat begins to separate from bone (may take all day or overnight). Remove from heat. Remove ducks and any meat separated from bones. When cool to touch, remove duck meat from bones, and cut into small pieces. Store meat in the refrigerator. Pour liquid through a fine wire-mesh strainer, discarding solids. Chill liquid to solidify fat. Remove fat from liquid surface. Bring liquid to a boil, and add sliced carrots and next 4 ingredients. Boil until vegetables are barely cooked. Add duck meat and salt to taste. Combine hot egg noodles and butter. Place noodles in individual serving bowls, and serve soup over noodles. Serve with nachos, tortilla chips, or warm buttered flour tortillas.

Yield: 6 to 10 servings.

—Marianne and Bruce Prabel
Chadds Ford, Pennsylvania

Store soup and noodles separately in the refrigerator, and reheat together in the microwave. It also freezes well. If duck is not available, substitute venison or elk.

DU

Wild Goose-and-Onion Soup

Here's a recipe that makes great use of a roasted goose carcass. For best results, start with a plucked bird rather than one that's been skinned.

1½ quarts water
1 roasted goose carcass with pan
  drippings
4 large onions, halved
4 tablespoons butter or margarine
1 cup pale dry sherry
6 beef bouillon cubes
3 tablespoons Worcestershire sauce

1 tablespoon caraway seeds
1 to 2 dashes of hot sauce
Salt and pepper to taste
Dark pumpernickel-rye bread slices,
  toasted
Swiss cheese
Grated Parmesan cheese

Simmer 1½ quarts water in the roasting pan the goose was cooked in. Loosen the browned particles from the bottom of the pan with a spoon. Add the browned skin that was not served during the carving, the leg bones, and the wing bones with remaining meat on them. Break up the carcass bones with the skin from the back, and add to the broth. Bring to a boil; reduce heat, and simmer 3 to 4 hours. Let cool, and remove all remaining meat from the bones, discarding bones and skin. Cut onion halves into ⅛-inch thick slices. Melt butter in a skillet, and add onion; sauté until golden brown. Add onion, sherry, and next 5 ingredients to the duck stock; simmer 20 to 30 minutes. Place 1 bread slice in each ovenproof serving bowl. Top each with 1 Swiss cheese slice. Broil each bowl 1 to 2 minutes or until cheese is melted. Serve soup over the bread slices. Top each serving with Parmesan cheese, if desired.

—Philip Whitford
Montello, Wisconsin

Goose Noodle Soup

1 small boneless goose breast, cut
   into small cubes
1 cup diced onion
1 cup diced celery
8 cups water

6 beef bouillon cubes
1 can beef bouillon (optional)
½ to ¾ bag large egg noodles
Salt and pepper to taste

Cook goose cubes and onion in a skillet until goose is browned. Combine goose, onion, celery, and next 3 ingredients in a slow cooker, and cook on HIGH 5 hours. Add noodles, and cook until tender. Salt and pepper to taste. Serve with crackers.

—*Harold E. Neameyer*
Bismarck, North Dakota

To make this soup

more festive, use

farfalle (bow tie pasta)

or conchiglie (seashell

pasta).

DU

45

Vegetable-Goose-Barley Soup

For a Cuban swing to this classic soup, substitute 1 (15.5-ounce) can black beans for kidney beans. Drain the beans, and add ¼ teaspoon chili powder or ground red pepper.

1 boneless skinless goose breast, cut into 3-inch cubes
2 tablespoons vegetable oil
1 large onion
6 whole cloves
⅓ cup diced carrot
⅓ cup diced celery
⅓ cup diced potato
½ green bell pepper, diced
1 (15.5-ounce) can kidney beans, drained

1 (10-ounce) can tomatoes, chopped
2 (14.5-ounce) cans beef broth
1 quart water
⅔ cup barley
4 garlic cloves
2 beef bouillon cubes
1 tablespoon Worcestershire sauce
2 teaspoons salt
1 teaspoon pepper
1 dried red chile pepper

Brown goose cubes in hot oil in a large stockpot. Stick cloves into onion. Add onion, carrot, and remaining ingredients to stockpot; simmer 2 hours.

Yield: This recipe serves a gaggle of hungry hunters.

—*Richard L. Weber*
Schaumburg, Illinois

Wild Turkey Soup

Leftover turkey, cubed
3 or 4 potatoes, cubed
1 large onion, chopped
1 or 2 carrots, grated
1 or 2 celery stalks, diced
½ green bell pepper, chopped

½ red bell pepper, chopped
½ yellow bell pepper, chopped
1 banana pepper, chopped
¼ cup apple cider vinegar
Salt and pepper to taste

Combine all ingredients in a large Dutch oven. Fill with water; bring to boil. Cover, reduce heat, and simmer 2 hours. More won't hurt, or put in crockpot. Simmer on low all day.

—James A. "Captain JAG" Gebde
Lesage, West Virginia

After serving a roasted or smoked turkey, pick the bones clean. The small pieces of meat from the bones are tender essentials to this soup. You can also prepare this recipe in a slow cooker. Simply let it simmer on LOW all day.

DU

Hearty Venison Soup

Serve this soup very
hot. When the fat in
venison cools, it hard-
ens quickly. It's always
wise to serve venison
on hot plates or bowls.

2 to 2½ pounds venison, cubed
1 beef bouillon cube
1 bay leaf
2 whole cloves
1 quart water
2 potatoes, chopped
2 celery stalks, chopped
1 can whole kernel corn

2 cans tomatoes
2 teaspoons salt
1 tablespoon dried parsley flakes
2 carrots, chopped
1 large onion, chopped
1 can peas
1 to 2 quarts water
¼ teaspoon pepper

Combine first 5 ingredients in a large Dutch oven, and simmer 30 minutes. Add potato
and remaining ingredients, and simmer 30 minutes or until vegetables are done.

Yields: 8 to 10 servings.

—Stanley Lubinski
Stevens Point, Wisconsin

48

Easy Fish Chowder

3 quarts water
4 pounds fresh fish fillets
4 tablespoons salt
2 (1-ounce) envelopes dry
   onion soup mix

2 boxes scalloped potatoes
2 (12-ounce) cans evaporated milk
1 tablespoon black pepper
1 (12-ounce) can tomato paste

Bring water to a boil in a large stockpot; add fish and salt. Boil 10 to 15 minutes or until fish flakes easily with a fork. Remove fish from stockpot, and flake. Add soup mix and next 4 ingredients to the fish stock, and simmer 30 minutes. Add fish, and simmer 10 minutes; serve hot.

—*Mary Debus*
Bella Vista, Arizona

Fish chowder often demands much from a busy cook. The beauty of this recipe is that it is easily prepared in your kitchen at home or in the most primitive camp conditions.

DU

49

Cheese-Fish Chowder

American cheese
may be substituted
in this recipe. Avoid
using Cheddar, since
it will curdle.

4 to 5 potatoes, diced
1 medium onion, finely chopped
3 celery stalks, finely chopped
Salt
Pepper
1 pound crappie, bluegill, bass, or
    white bass fillets (strip the fillets
    if they are large)

½ (8-ounce) process cheese spread
    loaf, cut into small pieces
2 to 3 cups milk
3 tablespoons butter or margarine

Combine first 3 ingredients in a large stockpot. Add water to a depth of 1 inch above the vegetables. Bring to a boil; reduce heat to medium. Add 4 shakes of pepper and 8 shakes of salt, and cook until potato is done. Add fish fillets, and cook until fillets are poached. Add cheese slowly, stirring until melted. Add milk to reach desired consistency. Add butter, and increase heat but do not boil. Cook until thoroughly heated. Serve immediately.

Yield: 4 to 6 servings.

—Gary E. Kaufman
Rockford, Illinois

Redfish Court Bouillon

1 (5-pound) redfish, scaled and
   gutted with head on
Salt, red pepper, and black pepper
   to taste
1 cup peanut oil
2 cups water
2 large onions, finely chopped
3 celery stalks, finely chopped
1 small bell pepper, finely chopped
4 lemons
1 (6-ounce) can tomato paste

½ (5-ounce) can diced tomatoes
   and green chiles
2 tablespoons Worcestershire sauce
1 tablespoon sugar
2 garlic cloves, finely chopped
6 bay leaves
½ cup flour
1 cup water
1 bunch green onions,
   finely chopped
1 bunch parsley, finely chopped

For best results, cook over an open campfire. Serve this delectable fish soup with a mixed green salad and hot garlic bread.

Filet redfish, leaving skin attached, and cut into 3-inch strips. Season with salt, red pepper, and black pepper to taste; set aside. Bring fish bones, head, 2 tablespoons oil, and 2 cups water to a boil in a large skillet; boil 1 hour. Remove from heat, debone meat, and pour stock through a wire-mesh strainer; set aside. Combine remaining peanut oil, onion, celery, and bell pepper in skillet; sauté 30 minutes or until onion is clear. Add fish stock, juice from 2 lemons, tomato paste, next 5 ingredients; simmer 2 hours. Add flour and water as needed to maintain desired consistency. Add seasoned fish strips, and cook 20 to 30 more minutes. Add green onions and 2 lemons, sliced, and cook 5 more minutes. Remove bay leaves, and discard. Sprinkle with chopped parsley before serving.

Yield: 6 to 8 servings.

—Ed Villien
Lafayette, Louisiana

DU

51

Spiced Goose Marinade

Marinades used on meat, poultry, and fish contain raw juices. If you brush them on during cooking, only do so during the early stages so they will have time to cook.

⅔ cup lemon juice
⅓ cup vegetable oil
⅛ teaspoon ground allspice
½ teaspoon ground ginger
½ teaspoon cayenne pepper
½ teaspoon garlic powder

½ teaspoon onion powder
¼ teaspoon hot sauce
3 teaspoons Durkee Red Hot Sauce
Boneless goose breasts, cut
   into strips
Water

Combine lemon juice and next 8 ingredients, stirring well. Place goose strips in a shallow dish, and add marinade. Add water only if goose is not covered completely. Cover, and marinate at least 24 hours.

—*Bruce A. Rickerson*
Delevan, New York

54

Oriental Mustard Goose Marinade

½ cup vegetable oil
½ cup prepared mustard
5 tablespoons vinegar
½ tablespoon dried red pepper flakes
½ tablespoon salt
1 tablespoon dried onion flakes
½ tablespoon brown sugar
½ teaspoon minced garlic

2 tablespoons dried parsley flakes
4 tablespoons soy sauce (optional)
Goose, cut into 1-inch strips
⅓ cup prepared mustard
⅓ cup ketchup
⅓ cup Bull's Eye Barbecue sauce
1 tablespoon coarsely ground red
  pepper

Combine first 9 ingredients and, if desired, soy sauce in a large bowl or zip-top plastic bag. Add marinade, and let marinate overnight. Barbecue according to desired method, basting with marinade. Combine ⅓ cup mustard and next 3 ingredients. Serve goose with mustard dipping sauce.

—*Earl Dunnigan*
Bismarck, North Dakota

Don't be tempted to use this marinade as a dipping sauce, since it contains raw juices. Try the recommended mustard sauce. It's easy to prepare and quite tasty.

Garlic-Shallot Sauce

When grilling with sweet sauces, brush the sauce on during the last 10 to 15 minutes. This allows the flavor to penetrate the food without burning.

1 stick butter or margarine
½ cup minced shallots
2 teaspoons minced garlic
1 cup heavy cream
Lemon pepper

Melt butter in a saucepan, and add garlic. Cook until garlic "pops." Add shallots, and cook until tender. Reduce heat to medium low. Add cream slowly until desired sauce consistency is reached. Add lemon pepper to taste.

—Jack R. Carter
Minneapolis, Minnesota

Cranberry Sauce

½ cup sugar mix (white, dark brown, or light brown)
1 cup Burgundy
1 (1½-inch) orange rind strip
1 (3-inch) cinnamon stick
1 bag cranberries

Combine sugar and wine, stirring to dissolve sugar. Add orange rind, cinnamon stick, and cranberries. Bring to a boil; cover, reduce heat, and simmer 15 to 20 minutes or until cranberries break open. Let cool; remove rind and cinnamon stick, discarding cinnamon stick. Cut rind into thin strips. Add rind strips to sauce; chill until firm.

—Karl Kaiser
Scottsdale, Arizona

Versatile Orange Glaze

½ pheasant
Whole milk
1 tablespoon butter or margarine
2 tablespoons orange marmalade
  with rind
1 tablespoon frozen orange juice
  concentrate

1 tablespoon Mexican vanilla
1 to 2 tablespoons teriyaki marinade
  and sauce
2 to 3 dashes hot sauce
Garlic salt to taste

Place pheasant in a glass bowl, and cover with whole milk. Chill 30 minutes. Cook butter and next 6 ingredients in a small saucepan over low heat until thoroughly heated. Remove pheasant from milk, and pat dry with paper towels. Place pheasant on an aluminum foil-covered baking sheet, and coat with glaze. Cook at 375° for 45 minutes to 1 hour, basting often. Reserve remaining sauce.

—*Art Wilkirson*
Tyler, Texas

You can substitute 2 quail (split up the back), 2 chicken legs and thighs, or 2 bone-in chicken breasts for pheasant. Serve the orange-glazed bird with rice, vegetables, and a good Merlot.

DU

Barbecue Sauce for Beef or Venison

*Creating barbecue
sauce from scratch is
neither time consuming
nor complicated.*

1 medium bottle of ketchup
⅛ cup cider vinegar
½ cup brown sugar
1 tablespoon Worcestershire sauce
½ teaspoon dry mustard
½ (1-ounce) envelope dry onion
   soup mix
Beef or venison
1 onion, thinly sliced (optional)

Cook first 6 ingredients in a saucepan over medium heat until thoroughly heated. Place meat in a 13- x 9-inch baking dish, and add sauce. Bake at 200° for at least 1½ hours. Add onion slices, if desired, and bake 2 more hours.

—Dona J. Berge
Dixon, Illinois

Zippy Barbecue Sauce

2 sticks butter or margarine
Chopped celery
Chopped bell pepper
Chopped onion
1¼ cups lemon juice
½ cup Worcestershire sauce
1 can chicken broth
2 tablespoons cornstarch, mixed
   with enough water to make a paste
1 lemon, sliced
Garlic powder
Paul Prudhomme's Magic Seasoning
Dried crushed red pepper
Hot sauce
Chopped fresh parsley

Melt butter in a large saucepan. Add a handful each of chopped celery, bell pepper, and onion. Add lemon juice and next 4 ingredients. Add garlic powder and next 3 ingredients to taste. Simmer 20 minutes; add parsley. This sauce is great for smoking crabs or basting seafood and vegetables on the grill.

—J. T. "Dr. Pulldoo" Dibble
Spring, Texas

58

Goose Gravy

2 cups flour
Water or cooking wine
2 boneless goose breasts, cubed
3 or 4 potatoes, cubed
1 large onion, chopped
1 or 2 carrots, grated
1 or 2 celery stalks, sliced

½ cup frozen peas, thawed
4 green onions, chopped
¼ cup apple cider vinegar
⅛ teaspoon chopped garlic
1 teaspoon paprika
Cayenne pepper to taste (optional)
Salt and pepper to taste

This gravy is so satisfying that it's almost a meal in itself. Serve it over rice, noodles, cornbread, and biscuits.

Combine flour and enough water to make a thin gravy in a large bowl. Combine gravy, goose, and remaining ingredients in a large stockpot. Bring to a boil, stirring constantly. Cover, reduce heat, and simmer 2 hours, stirring occasionally. Cook uncovered after simmering to thicken, if desired. You can also prepare this recipe in a slow cooker; simmer on LOW all day.

—James A. "Captain JAG" Gehde
Lesage, West Virginia

DU

Spicy Chutney with Tomato

Chutneys are flavorful Indian relishes. This one packs a punch with red pepper, fresh ginger, and garlic. Try it with grilled game or broiled waterfowl.

½ teaspoon mustard seeds
⅛ teaspoon cumin seeds
1 tablespoon vegetable oil
½ teaspoon minced garlic
½ teaspoon minced ginger

2 cups finely chopped seeded
  fresh tomatoes
½ teaspoon ground red pepper
⅛ teaspoon ground turmeric
1 teaspoon salt
1 teaspoon fresh lemon juice

In a covered medium frying pan heat mustard and cumin seeds in oil over medium-high heat. When mustard seeds begin to pop, turn heat down to medium. Add garlic and ginger; stir for 30 seconds. Add tomato and simmer for 2 to 3 minutes. Add red pepper, turmeric, and salt and fry until tomatoes are well cooked and broken up. Stir frequently to prevent sticking. Add lemon juice and remove from heat.

Yield: 1½ cups

—*Sean Wayne*
West Lafayette, Indiana

Waterfowl

Where else would we go to find the best recipes for ducks and geese than to members of Ducks Unlimited? They've been cooking waterfowl for generations, and believe me, they know what they're doing. Some of these recipes endure as family traditions or long-time duck club staples, others are newfangled and more innovative than you'll find in any other cookbook. Hang onto your taste buds, folks, and get ready to learn from the masters.

—*Billy Joe Cross*

Duck Fajitas

Mallards or teal are best for this recipe. However, since the meat is heavily marinated, other ducks also work well.

½ cup olive oil
⅓ cup lemon juice
⅓ cup soy sauce
⅓ cup Italian dressing
6 garlic cloves, minced
½ teaspoon dried sage
½ teaspoon ground cumin
1 teaspoon chili powder
½ teaspoon ground black pepper
2 pounds duck breast fillets

4 plum tomatoes, diced
1 white onion, finely chopped
⅓ cup fresh cilantro, minced
1 to 3 jalapeño peppers, minced
2 avocados, mashed
2 tablespoons lemon juice
2 tablespoons sour cream
1 dozen flour tortillas
2 cups (8 ounces) grated Cheddar cheese

Combine first 9 ingredients in a shallow dish, stirring well. Add duck, adding cold water if necessary for marinade to cover meat. Chill 1 hour or overnight. Combine tomato and next 3 ingredients in a small bowl; chill at least 30 minutes. Combine avocado, lemon juice, and sour cream, stirring well. Remove duck from marinade, reserving marinade. Grill duck over high heat (400° to 450°), basting with marinade. Slice duck into ¼-inch-wide strips. Microwave tortillas between two plates at HIGH 1 minute. Allow individuals to prepare their own fajitas using duck, tomato mixture, avocado mixture, tortillas, and cheese.

Yield: 4 servings.

—David M. Brown
Plano, Texas

Duck, Rosemary, and Wild Rice Pasty

¼ cup flour
2 teaspoons salt
1 teaspoon pepper
4 large duck fillets
3 tablespoons butter or margarine
1 tablespoon olive oil
1½ tablespoons dried crushed
  rosemary
1 cup beef broth
1 cup diced potato

1½ cup sliced carrot
1 cup celery, finely chopped
1 cup onion, finely chopped
1 tablespoon chopped shallots
  or garlic
1 tablespoon Worcestershire sauce
3 cups cooked wild rice
1 (15-ounce) package refrigerated
  piecrusts
Butter or margarine

Combine flour, salt, and pepper; dredge duck in flour mixture. Heat butter and oil in a heavy skillet over medium-high heat. Add duck, and brown 2 minutes on each side, sprinkling with rosemary as it browns. Remove duck from pan, and slice into ¼-inch strips. Add ½ cup beef broth, potato, and carrot to skillet, and cook 3 minutes. Add celery, onion, and shallots, and cook 3 more minutes, adding more broth if necessary to prevent sticking. Return duck to skillet, and add Worcestershire sauce, rice, and remaining ½ cup beef broth. Fit 1 piecrust into a 10-inch deep-dish pieplate according to package directions. Spoon duck mixture into prepared piecrust. Dot with butter, and top with remaining piecrust, cutting several slits in top. Bake at 425° for 10 minutes; reduce heat to 350°, and bake 40 minutes or until lightly browned.

—June Swentkofske
Cohasset, Minnesota

Pasties originated in Cornwall County, England, where lead and tin miners carried the meal into collieries. Easily transported, this hearty pie encloses meat in a baked pastry crust.

DU

Cajun Pot Roast Duck

Chef Williams Marinade

adds tremendous flavor

and maintains the

delicate moisture balance

in this low-fat recipe.

The injector (syringe) is

becoming a very popular

kitchen tool in Louisiana

because of its versatility.

1 large duck	1 large yellow onion
Seasoned salt	2 potatoes, cubed
Hot sauce	2 carrots
Chef Williams Cajun Injector Marinade	2 celery stalks, sliced
	1 cup white wine
Seasoning injector	2 tablespoons hot sauce

Season duck with seasoned salt and hot sauce. Fill the seasoning injector with marinade, and stick the syringe in the middle of the breast, next to the breastbone. Slide syringe to the wishbone. Gently inject the marinade, backing up slowly to the starting point. Be sure to maintain constant feeding of the seasoning as you move. Do not remove injector at the initial point. Turn the needle, and continue down the breastbone towards the rump. Feed the marinade as you back all the way out. Inject the leg and thigh in the same manner. Repeat the injection process on the other half of the duck. Chill 2 to 3 days, if desired. If you are not in a hurry, letting the duck marinate a long time adds flavor to the meat; however, when you gotta cook, you gotta cook. Place duck in a large Dutch oven, and add onion and next 3 ingredients. Add 1 cup marinade, wine, and hot sauce. Cover and simmer 1 hour or until tender. Serve over rice and with cornbread for sopping.

Yield: 4 servings.

—*Markle Farber*
Lake Charles, Louisiana

Duck Gumbo

½ cup vegetable oil
1 cup flour
½ cup chopped green bell pepper
1½ cups chopped yellow onion
¼ cup chopped celery
1 pound chopped pork tasso,
   optional
1 pound smoked sausage
2 garlic cloves, chopped

4 quarts boiling water
2 bay leaves (crushed)
2 ducks
2 to 3 teaspoons hot sauce
1 cup chopped green onions
Seasoned salt
Hot cooked Louisiana rice
Filé powder

Cook oil and flour in a cast-iron Dutch oven over medium-low heat, stirring constantly, 30 to 45 minutes or until dark brown. Add bell pepper, onion, and celery, and sauté 2 to 4 minutes. Add tasso, smoked sausage, and garlic, and cook 1 minute. Add 4 quarts water, bay leaves, and duck, stirring well. Reduce heat, and simmer 1 hour and 30 minutes to 2 hours, stirring every 10 to 15 minutes. Add hot sauce, green onions, and seasoned salt during the last 15 minutes. Serve over rice, and sprinkle with filé.

Yield: 4 to 6 servings.

—*Markle Farber*
Lake Charles, Louisiana

Gumbo gets its name from okra, which is a vegetable used for thickening and flavor. While this recipe does not call for okra pods, you will love the combination of French, Spanish, and Indian cuisines.

DU

Teal and Oyster Gumbo

Feel free to substitute other ducks for teal. Because teal are small, decrease the number of birds used in this recipe if using a large species, such as mallards.

6 teal, cut into pieces
Salt, red pepper, and black pepper
    to taste
2 cups flour
2 cups vegetable oil
2 onion, finely chopped
1 celery stalk, finely chopped
2 bell peppers, chopped
1 pound butter or margarine
6 cups cold water
4 dozen raw oysters
1 bunch green onion tops, finely
    chopped
1 bunch fresh parsley, finely
    chopped

Season teal with salt, red pepper, and black pepper to taste. Brown teal in a heavy skillet. Remove teal from skillet, and drain excess grease; cut duck into pieces. Cook flour and oil in a large Dutch oven over low heat, stirring constantly, 20 to 30 minutes or until almost black. Add onion and next 3 ingredients, and cook until tender. Add 6 cups cold water, stirring well. Add duck, and cook over low heat 2 hours and 30 minutes or until duck is tender, adding water if necessary to keep desired consistency. Add oysters, green onion, parsley, and half of oyster juice 20 minutes before serving. Serve with white rice, French bread, and potato salad.

Yield: 8 servings.

—Ed Villien
Lafayette, Louisiana

66

Duck 'n' Stuff

½ pound smoked pork sausage
⅓ pound pork tasso
¼ package frozen seasoning mix or
    1 small onion, minced (optional)
8 boneless duck breasts

1 tablespoon Worcestershire or
    soy sauce
Salt, pepper, and garlic salt to taste
1 package bacon

Process sausage and tasso in a food processor until smooth. Melt frozen seasoning mix in a skillet, and add sausage mixture. Cook over medium to low heat 15 minutes. Flatten duck breasts to ¼-inch thickness using a meat mallet. Rub meat with Worcestershire sauce and salt, pepper, and garlic salt to taste; chill 1 hour. Spread stuffing ¼-inch thick between matching breast pieces; wrap with bacon, and wrap tightly in aluminum foil. Place in a roasting pan, and bake at 350° for 40 minutes, opening foil during last 15 minutes to brown.

- *You can also cook this recipe over a pit. Secure bacon with wooden picks, and cook 30 minutes. Wrap in foil, and set aside on the grill until you're ready to eat (not too long, the duck may get tough).*

Yield: 4 servings.

—*Jesse Ludeau*
Ville Platte, Louisiana

Tasso is smoked and highly seasoned pork. Unless you live in Louisiana, you might have trouble finding tasso in your market. If so, omit it and simply use sausage.

Country Club-style Mallard

Currants are small seedless raisins produced mainly in California. Although currant jelly is preferred for this recipe, you may substitute brown sugar.

3 ducks
Salt and pepper to taste
6 celery stalks
1½ quarts well-seasoned bread
 stuffing
1 cup water
½ cup dry red wine
¼ cup orange marmalade

¼ cup currant jelly
1 orange, diced, rind and all
½ lemon, diced, rind and all
1 tablespoon browning-and-
 seasoning sauce
Dash tarragon
2 quarts well-seasoned chicken broth
Flour

Season duck with salt and pepper to taste, and place 2 celery stalks in each cavity. Bake duck, breast side up, at 450° for 30 minutes or until golden brown. Remove from oven, and reduce temperature to 400°. Remove celery, and drain blood and juices. Discard drippings. Fill duck with stuffing, and place, breast side down, in roasting pan. Add 1 cup water, next 7 ingredients, and enough broth to almost cover duck. Cover pan loosely with aluminum foil. Bake at 400° for 3 hours or until tender. Remove duck from pan, and keep warm. Skim fat off gravy. Bring gravy to a boil, and cook until reduced by half, thickening with flour as desired. Pour gravy through a wire-mesh strainer, and serve with duck.

Yield: 4 to 6 servings.

—Dan James
Larrabee, Iowa

Duck Breast Schnitzel

**2 boneless duck breasts, flattened
   to ⅛- to ¼-inch thickness**
Flour
1 egg, lightly beaten

Fine, dry breadcrumbs
Salt and pepper to taste
Butter or margarine

Dredge duck in flour, and dip in egg. Dredge in breadcrumbs. Salt and pepper to taste. Melt butter in a skillet over medium-high heat. Add duck, and fry until golden brown, turning once.

—*Col. Jack D. Rice*
Olympia, Washington

The originator of this meal immigrated to America from Germany, and she brought this recipe, using veal, with her. She and her husband perfected it for duck.

Filipino Adobo Duck

Here's an opportunity to turn your puddle ducks into a unique Filipino meal. Any puddler, such as a mallard, will work well in this delicious recipe.

2 puddle ducks, cut into fryer pieces
6 garlic cloves, chopped
2 tablespoons vegetable oil
2 cups water
¾ cup white vinegar
½ cup soy sauce
15 whole peppercorns
3 bay leaves

Sauté duck and garlic in hot oil in a skillet until duck is browned. Add 2 cups water, and remaining ingredients, and simmer, covered, 30 minutes. Remove duck, and set aside. Skim oil off the sauce, and simmer, uncovered, until reduced by half. Remove bay leaf, and discard. Serve duck over rice, and top with sauce.

—Richard L. Weber
Schaumburg, Illinois

Teriyaki Duck Kabobs

1 large onion
2 bell peppers
1 (8-ounce) package fresh
   mushrooms

8 large duck breast halves,
   cut into 1-inch cubes
Teriyaki marinade and sauce
Pepper to taste
Hot cooked wild rice

Cut onion, bell peppers, and mushrooms into 1-inch pieces. Combine vegetables and duck in a shallow dish, and cover with teriyaki sauce. Chill overnight. Alternate duck cubes and vegetable chunks on skewers, and season with pepper to taste. Grill over medium-high heat (350° to 400°) 10 minutes, basting often with teriyaki sauce. Serve with wild rice.

Yield: 4 servings or enough to feed 2 hungry hunters.

—*Clement Cravens*
New Madrid, Missouri

To ensure even grilling, leave $\frac{1}{4}$-inch gap between duck and vegetables.

71

Mexi-Baked Duck

For a spicier dish, include 2 dashes of hot sauce, such as Tabasco, when adding the seasonings.

2 to 3 skinless duck breasts and legs
Salt and pepper to taste
4 tablespoons flour
⅓ cup vegetable oil
1 small onion, sliced
1 medium-size green bell pepper, chopped

¾ cup regular rice
2½ cups vegetable juice
2 tablespoons ketchup
1 teaspoon dried sage
1 teaspoon ground cumin
Garnishes: sliced ripe olives, fresh orange slices

Season duck with salt and pepper to taste, and dredge in flour. Brown duck in hot oil in a skillet. Remove duck from skillet, and place in a 13- x 9-inch baking dish. Add onion, bell pepper, and rice to drippings, and sauté 10 minutes. Add vegetable juice and next 3 ingredients, and bring to a boil; boil 10 minutes. Pour onion mixture over duck. Bake, covered, at 350° for 1 hour and 30 minutes, adding water as needed to keep moist. Garnish if desired.

—Mrs. Karen Standal
Bonners Ferry, Idaho

Microwaved Duck with Lentils

1 duck, raised and patted dry
1 onion, sliced
½ cup lentils, rinsed and drained
1 tablespoon fresh thyme leaves
4 cups chicken or beef stock broth
¼ cup tomato paste

1 tablespoon balsamic vinegar
1½ teaspoon salt
½ teaspoon paprika
Freshly ground black pepper, to
taste

Cut the duck into pieces; remove and discard the backbone. Remove the wings and split them at the "elbow." Remove the legs, and separate the drumsticks from the thighs. Halve each breast. Arrange the pieces in a 3-quart microwave-safe casserole. Cook at full power, 650 to 700 watts, uncovered, for 2½ minutes. Rearrange the pieces, and cook another 2½ minutes. Discard any liquid that has accumulated in the casserole. Add the onion, lentils, and thyme. Stir the remaining ingredients together in small bowl, and pour this mixture over the duck. Cover, and cook for 45 minutes. Let stand for 5 minutes before serving.

—Veronica Quinn
Louisville, Kentucky

To ensure even cooking, prepare this meal in a carousel microwave. If a carousel is not available, rotate the casserole periodically while cooking.

DU

73

Fried Rice with Duck

Fried rice, or "chow fan," has become an American favorite. Season this Oriental classic with low-sodium soy sauce immediately before serving.

1 tablespoon dry sherry
1 tablespoon cornstarch
2 cups ½-inch-thick duck breast strips
½ cup diced onion
½ cup diced celery
4 tablespoons vegetable oil
1 tablespoon soy sauce

2 tablespoons boiling water
¼ cup sliced fresh mushrooms
1 piece fresh gingerroot, sliced
1 garlic clove
3 cups cooked long-grain rice, chilled
½ cup diced ham
3 eggs, lightly beaten

Combine sherry and cornstarch in a small bowl; dip duck strips in mixture to coat. Stir-fry onion and celery in 2 tablespoons hot oil in a wok 2 minutes, shaking wok to prevent browning. Add soy sauce and 2 tablespoons water. Reduce heat to medium; cover and cook 1 minute. Add mushrooms; cover and cook 1 to 2 minutes or until tender. Remove vegetables from wok, and set aside. Sauté ginger and garlic in remaining 2 tablespoons hot oil in wok until browned. Remove ginger and garlic, and discard. Add duck to wok, and stir-fry 2 minutes. Add cooked vegetables, rice, and diced ham to wok. Toss until hot. Make a well in center of mixture, and add additional oil if needed. Pour eggs in center, and cook until scrambled, stirring constantly.

Yield: 4 servings

—*Michael T. Hogan*
Mina, South Dakota

Duck Teriyaki Stir-Fry with Cashews

½ cup dry white or red wine
¼ cup vegetable oil
¼ cup teriyaki sauce
2 garlic cloves, pressed or minced
2 skinless boneless ducks, cut into
⅛-inch strips
1 tablespoon vegetable oil
1 pound fresh broccoli, cut into
bite-size pieces or ½ pound fresh
or frozen snow pea pods

1 cup bean sprouts
1 medium carrot, shredded
1 (8-ounce) can water chestnuts,
drained
1 (8-ounce) can bamboo shoots,
drained
½ cup cashews
Hot cooked white or brown rice

Don't omit the snow peas because they add a crisp, lightly sweet taste to this delicious meal.

Combine first 4 ingredients in a glass bowl, and add duck. Chill 8 hours or overnight, stirring occasionally. Remove duck from marinade, reserving marinade. Stir-fry duck in hot oil in a wok until desired degree of doneness; remove duck from wok, and keep warm. Add ¼ cup reserved marinade, broccoli, and next 4 ingredients to wok; stir-fry until broccoli is crisp-tender. Return duck to wok, and add cashews. Cook until thoroughly heated. Serve over rice.

Yield: 4 to 6 servings.

—Brian Burke
Kenmore, New York

Oriental Fried Duck

**6 to 8 duck breasts, flattened
 to ¼-inch thickness and
 cut into strips**
1 tablespoon Worcestershire sauce
½ cup Italian dressing
1 tablespoon soy sauce
1 tablespoon Chinese mustard
1 tablespoon Chinese duck sauce
Ground allspice
2 cups flour
Salt and pepper to taste
Vegetable oil

Combine first 6 ingredients in a shallow dish, and chill overnight. Remove duck from marinade, discarding marinade. Sprinkle with allspice. Dredge duck in flour, and season with salt and pepper to taste. Fry in hot oil 4 to 5 minutes on each side or until done.

Yield: 4 to 5 servings.

—*Karl Voorhees*
Monroe, Louisiana

You don't have to save your leftover Chinese mustard from Oriental take-out deliveries. Most supermarkets carry it in the mustard or International sections of the store.

Grilled Sesame Duck Filets

½ cup soy sauce
½ cup vegetable oil
¼ cup water
2 tablespoons minced onion
⅛ teaspoon ground red pepper
2 tablespoons sesame seeds

1 tablespoon sugar
¾ teaspoon salt
½ teaspoon minced garlic
8 duck breast fillets
8 bacon slices

Combine first 9 ingredients in a shallow dish, stirring well. Add duck, and chill 4 to 8 hours, turning duck occasionally. Drain duck, reserving marinade. Wrap 1 bacon slice around each breast, and secure with wooden picks. Grill, covered, over medium heat (300° to 350°) 6 to 8 minutes, basting with reserved marinade.

—*Cheralynn A. Schnepp*
Tucson, Arizona

Duck is naturally rich and flavorful. Don't dry out the tender meat by overcooking it. Test the meat by pricking with a sharp knife. Juices should appear yellow, not pink.

DU

Individual Duck Wellington

Irish chefs developed
beef Wellington in honor
of the Duke of
Wellington, who
defeated Napoleon in
the battle of 1815. You'll
love this Wellington with
duck. Try it with goose,
too, and allow it to cook
10 additional minutes.

8 duck breast halves
1 tablespoon vegetable oil
½ pound creamy liverwurst
½ cup chopped green onions
2 tablespoons chopped parsley

1 (17¼-ounce) package frozen puff
   pastry sheets, thawed
1 egg, lightly beaten
1 tablespoon water

Brown duck in hot oil; drain on paper towels, and chill. Preheat oven to 400°. Combine liverwurst, green onions, and parsley. Spoon evenly on top and sides of duck. Roll pastry out on a lightly floured surface into a 14-inch square; cut into 4 (7-inch) squares. Whisk together egg and 1 tablespoon water in a small bowl. Place duck evenly in squares, and brush pastry edges with egg mixture. Fold pastry over duck, pinching edges to seal. Place, seam side down, on an ungreased baking sheet. Bake at 400° for 25 minutes or until golden, covering with aluminum foil during last 5 minutes to prevent excessive browning.

Yield: 8 servings.

—Louise Scott
Miami, Florida

Microwave Barbecue Duck Breasts

¼ cup white vinegar
½ cup tomato paste
3 tablespoons brown sugar
1 tablespoon onion powder
1 tablespoon chili powder

1 tablespoon Worcestershire sauce
½ tablespoon freshly ground pepper
½ tablespoon dry mustard
4 to 5 large boneless duck breasts

Combine first 8 ingredients in a bowl, stirring well. Add duck, and chill 4 to 5 hours. Remove duck from marinade, reserving marinade. Chill marinade, and place duck in a single layer in a microwave-safe dish. Cover loosely, and microwave at MEDIUM HIGH (80% power) 10 to 12 minutes. Remove from microwave; cover tightly, and let stand at room temperature 5 minutes before serving. Microwave marinade at HIGH 2 minutes, stirring once. Serve marinade with duck.

—*Jim Waldman*
Houston, Texas

Duck continues to cook after removing it from heat. It is important to let the bird sit 5 minutes before serving it. Don't forget to return the sauce to the refrigerator while microwaving the bird. This sauce has raw juice in it, so cook it thoroughly.

DU

Beer Barbecue Duck

¾ cup bock or honey wheat beer
1 cup ketchup
¼ cup honey
¼ cup Worcestershire sauce
2 teaspoons salt
½ teaspoon paprika

¼ teaspoon cayenne pepper
¼ teaspoon white pepper
¼ teaspoon black pepper
½ teaspoon garlic powder
1 teaspoon dried onion flakes
2 ducks or 4 duck breasts

Cook first 4 ingredients in a medium saucepan over medium heat until honey is dissolved. Add salt and next 6 ingredients, stirring well. Reduce heat, and simmer 20 to 30 minutes. Cook duck according to desired method using beer mixture to marinate, to baste, or as a sauce.

—*Brian J. Donovan*
Austin, Texas

Braised Duck Italian

2 wild ducks, cut into pieces
Bacon fat
1 large yellow onion, coarsely
   chopped
3 medium carrots, cut crosswise
   into ¼-inch slices
2 celery stalks, cut crosswise
   into ½-inch slices

Olive oil
1½ cups pitted ripe olives,
   coarsely chopped
Dried thyme
Dried parsley flakes
Salt and pepper to taste
⅓ bottle hearty red wine
Hot cooked wild rice

Brown duck in hot bacon fat in a skillet, turning frequently. Remove duck from skillet, and wipe skillet with a paper towel. Cook onion, carrot, and celery in hot oil until tender. Add olives and next 3 ingredients, and cook until blended, stirring often. Add duck and red wine, stirring thoroughly. Cook, covered, until meat is light pink not brown. Serve with rice.

—Bernard J. Ridder, Jr.
Long Beach, California

If you are looking for a unique, savory way to prepare duck, try this easy braised method. Any duck species will work—even shovelers. Leftovers can be stored in the refrigerator and reheated the next day.

81

Pot-Roasted Duck

Here's a quick duck recipe that doesn't require much time in the kitchen. While you wait for the birds to cook, you have plenty of time to review your days in the duck blind.

2 large ducks or 4 small ducks
4 garlic cloves
Salt and pepper to taste

Vegetable oil
4 large onions, chopped

Make 1 hole in each side of the duck breasts; place 1 garlic clove in each hole. Season duck inside and out with salt and pepper to taste. Brown duck in hot oil in a cast-iron skillet over medium heat. Remove duck from skillet, and set aside. Cook onion in skillet until browned. Return duck to skillet, breast side down, and add enough water to cover breasts. Cook until duck is tender and gravy is thickened, adding more water as needed. This process takes at least 4 hours if the ducks are tough.

—*Gordon and Marie Steele*
Hemphill, Texas

Duck à la Margaret

1 duck
Chopped celery
Chopped apple
1 (12-ounce) can cola or
    lemon-lime soft drink
¼ cup butter or margarine
4 tablespoons flour

½ teaspoon salt
2 tablespoons strawberry jam
¼ cup granulated sugar
1 tablespoon brown sugar
1 small can frozen orange juice
    concentrate, thawed
2 jiggers red or white wine

Soak duck overnight in saltwater. Wash and clean out duck cavity; stuff with celery and apple. Place duck in a roasting pan, and add water to a depth of 2 inches. Bake, covered, at 300° for 2 hours. Drain off grease, and add soft drink. Bake 1 hour and 30 minutes. Melt butter in a small saucepan; add flour and salt, stirring well. Add jam and next 4 ingredients, and bring to a boil. Boil, stirring constantly, until thickened. Serve sauce over duck.

—Margaret Lavallee
St. Ambroise, Manitoba

Duck's rich flavor is accentuated by sauces, especially those with acidic citrus flavor. Here is a classic orange sauce that perfectly complements this baked bird.

DU

Simply Elegant Raspberry Duck

Quick, easy, and delicious—what more could you ask for in a duck recipe? To enhance the delicate, sweet flavors, mallards or teal are recommended.

2 wild ducks
Salt and pepper to taste
1 (8-ounce) package frozen
   raspberries, thawed

½ cup sugar
3 tablespoons cornstarch
¼ cup lemon juice
1 cup white wine

Season duck with salt and pepper to taste. Puree raspberries in a blender. Combine raspberries, sugar, and next 3 ingredients in a saucepan. Bring to a boil, and cook until thickened. Bake duck at 350° for 1 hour; reduce heat to 300°, and bake 1 more hour, basting with raspberry sauce during last 30 minutes. Serve with remaining raspberry sauce.

Yield: 4 servings.

—*Michael Farias*
Laredo, Texas

Roasted Duck with Cranberry Merlot Sauce

2 medium ducks
Salt and pepper to taste
1 orange, cut into small pieces
1 apple, chopped
¼ cup dried cranberries
½ cup water

2 shallots, minced
Vegetable oil
½ cup Merlot
1 can fat-free chicken stock
¼ cup balsamic vinegar
Pinch of dried thyme

Season duck with salt and pepper to taste, and fill cavity with orange and apple. Grill over medium heat (300° to 350°) until medium well. Bring cranberries and ½ cup water to a boil in a small saucepan. Remove from heat, and let soften 10 minutes. Drain cranberries, reserving liquid. Brown shallots in hot oil in a skillet. Add Merlot, and bring to a boil. Reduce heat, and simmer 10 minutes or until reduced by half. Add chicken stock; bring to a boil. Add liquid from cranberries; bring to a boil. Reduce heat, and simmer until reduced by half. Add balsamic vinegar, thyme, and salt and pepper to taste; bring to a boil. Reduce heat, and simmer until reduced by half. Add cranberries, and cook 1 to 2 minutes or until thoroughly heated. Serve cranberry sauce with duck.

—Aurora P. Stelz
Falls Church, Virginia

Oranges aren't the only fruit that complements a duck's appealing flavor. Cranberries add zing to this roasted bird. Complete the meal with asparagus, wild rice with almonds, and a glass of Merlot.

Dusty's Roast Duck with Apple Gravy

4 wild Mallard ducks or
   1 Canada goose
¾ cup baking soda
¼ cup salt
Salt and pepper to taste
2 apples, quartered
2 onions, quartered
1 cup apple juice

1 cup water
Poultry seasoning
Garlic salt
Soy sauce
Chicken bouillon
Celery salt
Butter or margarine
Flour

Who is Dusty? She's the faithful hunting dog of the man who perfected this recipe. Without her, his freezer would only be half full. If a goose is in your freezer, use it and increase roasting time by almost 1 hour.

Soak duck overnight in sink in water to cover, baking soda, and salt. Remove ducks from water, and pat dry. Season duck cavity with salt and pepper to taste; stuff with apple and onion. Place duck, breast side down, in a large roasting pan. Add apple juice and next 6 ingredients, stirring well. Lightly butter duck, and season with salt and pepper to taste. Bake, covered, at 450° for 30 minutes. Reduce heat to 325°, and bake 2 hours and 30 minutes. Remove duck from pan. Skim fat from drippings. Add desired amount of flour to drippings to make gravy; bring to a boil. Cook until thickened.

—*Derek Getty*
Boyle, Alberta

Gramp's Roast Wild Duck

2 large ducks or 4 wood ducks
½ cup salt
½ cup apple cider vinegar

2 oranges, halved
Salt and pepper to taste
4 bacon slices

Soak duck in salt, vinegar, and water to cover 1 hour. Rinse duck, and place 1 orange half in each cavity; season with salt and pepper to taste. Place 1 bacon slice over each breast. Wrap birds individually in aluminum foil, and place, breast side up, in a roasting pan. Add water to a depth of ½ inch in pan. Bake at 325° for 2 hours and 30 minutes or until tender. Remove foil, orange, and bacon, and discard.

—*Stephen T. Craft*
Traverse City, Michigan

Rice is a natural side dish for this simple, delicious roast duck. You have to love a meal that "Gramps" endorses.

DU

Grilled Duck Breasts with Cherry Chutney

Chutney is a sweet-and-sour relish with fruit as a main ingredient. This chutney uses dried cherries, which can usually be found even when the fruit is not in season. Taste the chutney as it simmers. Add molasses if additional sweetness is desired.

4 tablespoons vegetable oil
1 tablespoon salt
2 tablespoons soy sauce
1 tablespoon sesame oil
1 tablespoon lemon pepper
1 tablespoon dried tarragon
4 duck breasts, with skin

2 cups broth (duck, beef, or chicken)
1 onion, chopped
1 cup sliced mushrooms
2 apples, peeled and chopped
4 ounces dried cherries
1 to 2 teaspoons molasses (optional)

Combine first 6 ingredients in a shallow dish. Add duck, stirring to coat. Chill at least 30 minutes. Cook broth in a saucepan; add onion, and bring to a boil. Boil, covered, 10 minutes. Add mushrooms and apple. Reduce heat, and simmer 10 minutes. Add cherries, and simmer 5 more minutes. Add molasses, if desired. Keep warm. Grill duck, covered, over high heat (450° to 500°) 7 minutes. Slice the meat diagonally and arrange on a plate. Pour the warm cherry chutney over the meat.

—R. David Farris
Portland, Oregon

Duck with Cilantro Butter

¼ **pound butter or margarine**
Juice of lime
3 garlic cloves, minced
¼ **cup minced cilantro**
Salt and pepper to taste
¼ **teaspoon cayenne pepper**

¼ **cup fresh lime juice**
¼ **cup canola oil**
3 tablespoons cilantro leaves
8 duck breasts
½ **teaspoon salt**
½ **teaspoon freshly ground pepper**

Combine butter and lime juice; add garlic and next 3 ingredients, stirring well. Transfer to plastic wrap; roll into a log, and chill overnight. Combine ¼ cup lime juice, oil, and cilantro in a small bowl. Season duck with salt and pepper. Dip breasts in lime marinade to coat, and chill overnight. Grill duck over medium heat (300° to 350°) 3 minutes on each side. Transfer to a warm platter, and serve with cilantro butter.

—*James L. Nelson*
Valparaiso, Indiana

Cilantro, fresh coriander, and Chinese parsley all refer to the same plant. In America, the seeds are known as coriander, while the herb's leaves are known as cilantro. You might recognize the leaves' sharp, fresh taste from salsa and other Mexican dishes.

DU

Grilled Pineapple Wood Ducks

Pineapple, while a tropical fruit, finds its way into countless dishes. Its sweet, juicy flavor offers the perfect balance for sweet-and-sour sauces. This grilled mixture leans toward the sweet side without being overpowering.

Blackened seasoning
Olive oil
Garlic salt
4 ducks, cleaned
1 cup duck broth
1 cup crushed pineapple
1 cup cooking wine
½ cup onion

2 (10½-ounce) cans condensed
  chicken broth
1 medium apple, sliced
¼ cup honey
¼ cup Worcestershire sauce
¼ cup butter or margarine
½ cup lemon juice
Salt and pepper to taste

Combine first 4 ingredients, and chill 1 hour. Remove duck from marinade, discarding marinade. Grill over medium-low heat (300° to 325°) 5 to 6 minutes on each side. Transfer duck to a 13- x 9-inch baking dish, and add broth, pineapple, and wine. Place apple on top and sides of duck. Bake at 350° for 45 to 55 minutes. Combine honey and next 4 ingredients in a small saucepan. Cook until thoroughly heated. Serve sauce hot with duck.

—*Larry D. Greene*
Eure, North Carolina

Goose Scampi

1 skinless goose breast, cut into
   bite-size pieces
2 garlic cloves, minced
1 teaspoon dry mustard
1 teaspoon salt
½ teaspoon pepper

4 tablespoons chopped fresh parsley
¼ teaspoon dried oregano leaves
¼ teaspoon dried basil leaves
4 tablespoons lemon juice
½ cup olive oil
½ cup Italian-seasoned breadcrumbs

Place goose in a 9-inch square pan. Combine garlic and next 8 ingredients, and pour over goose. Marinate at least 2 hours. Top with breadcrumbs, and bake at 350° for 1 hour or until tender.

—*Ernest Bugnet*
West Greenwich, Rhode Island

Scampi comes from the Italian word for shrimp. However, most Americans equate it with the dish that combines shrimp, garlic, and oil. Even when shrimp is not present in a garlic-oil-based recipe, we call it scampi.

DU

91

No-Dishes-To-Wash Jalapeño Goose

The name says it all. If you are looking for an easy-to-prepare meal with a kick, you have found it. For milder-tasting goose, seed and de-rib the jalapeño.

1 skinless goose
1 cup teriyaki sauce
1 cup tawny port
4 onions, chopped
2 celery stalks, chopped

4 apples, quartered
1 jalapeño pepper, sliced
1 teaspoon black pepper
1 teaspoon dried basil
½ cup minced garlic

Place goose, breast side down, in a pan made from 3 layers of aluminum foil. Add teriyaki sauce and next 3 ingredients. Place apple in goose cavity. Place jalapeño around goose. Season goose with pepper, basil, and garlic. Fold foil over goose, and seal tightly. Bake at 350° for 6 hours.

—*Noel Allan*
San Diego, California

Goose Braciola

1 goose
1 cup red wine
½ cup Parmesan cheese
½ cup soft breadcrumbs
1 egg

2 garlic cloves, minced
1 teaspoon dried oregano
Salt and pepper to taste
3 tablespoons olive oil
Favorite tomato sauce recipe

Fillet goose breasts, and cut lengthwise into ¼-inch-thick slices. Flatten slices to ⅛-inch thick, using a meat mallet, and place in a shallow dish. Add wine, and chill 30 minutes. Combine cheese and next 5 ingredients, stirring until a paste is formed. Remove goose from marinade, discarding marinade. Spread paste evenly on goose slices; roll up, jellyroll fashion, and secure with string. Sauté goose in hot oil in a large skillet until lightly browned. Transfer goose to saucepan with tomato sauce cooking, and cook 1 hour and 30 minutes to 2 hours. (If using a commercially prepared sauce, finish cooking braciola at least 1 hour in sauce.)

—*Gino Monaco*
Port Clinton, Ohio

Braciola is pronounced (brah-chee-OH-lah). Homemade tomato sauce works best in this dish, but commercially prepared sauce may be substituted. Serve this delicious meal with your favorite pasta and hot garlic bread.

DU

Green Chiles with Goose

Rotel is a brand of canned tomatoes with green chiles. Look for it in your supermarket with the canned tomatoes. If you can't find it, substitute 1 (14.5-ounce) can diced tomatoes and 2 to 3 additional fresh green chiles.

2 goose breasts, cut into small pieces
2 tablespoons flour
2 tablespoons vegetable oil
2 large onions, chopped
5 green chiles, diced, or
   1 (4.5-ounce) can diced
    green chiles

1 (10-ounce) can diced tomatoes
   with green chiles
1 cup water
1 teaspoon dried oregano
1 teaspoon ground cumin
1 teaspoon salt
1 teaspoon pepper
Fresh diced cilantro to taste

Dredge goose in flour, and brown in hot oil in a skillet. Add onion, and cook until tender. Add chiles and next 7 ingredients, and cook until thoroughly heated. Reduce heat, and simmer until ready to serve. Serve with warm tortillas.

—*J. T. Kelson*
Dalhart, Texas

94

Roast Goose Chili

1 tablespoon butter or margarine
1 cup onion, minced
1 garlic clove, minced
2 cups cubed goose
1 (16-ounce) can tomatoes
1 (16-ounce) can chili beans
1 cup green bell pepper, minced

1 cup beer
1 tablespoon chili powder
½ teaspoon salt
¼ teaspoon black pepper
½ teaspoon dried basil
1 teaspoon hot pepper sauce

Melt butter in a large heavy skillet over low heat; add onion and garlic, and sauté until golden brown. Add goose, and cook until lightly browned. Add tomatoes and remaining ingredients, and bring to a boil. Reduce heat, and simmer, uncovered, 3 hours or until sauce reaches desired thickness.

- *You can also prepare this in a slow cooker. After browning the onion, garlic, and goose, combine all ingredients in a slow cooker, and cook on LOW 8 to 10 hours.*

Yield: 4 servings

—Charlotte Dutton
Nanjemoy, Maryland

Here's is the perfect recipe to use up leftover roast goose. Remove all meat from the carcass, and cut it into small pieces. This slow method of cooking tenderizes even the most dry or tough bird.

Sauerkraut Baked Goose

1 wild goose
½ cup Burgundy
1 large can sauerkraut

Salt and pepper to taste
2 to 3 tablespoons cornstarch
⅓ cup cold water

This hearty meal uniquely incorporates sauerkraut in and around the roasted goose. Serve the bird with potatoes and vegetables.

Place goose in a large roasting pan, and add water to a depth of 1½ inches. Combine Burgundy and sauerkraut, and place ⅓ cup mixture in goose cavity. Add remaining Burgundy mixture to roasting pan. Season with salt and pepper to taste. Bake, covered, at 325° for 2 hours, basting occasionally. Remove goose from pan, and place on a serving platter. Skim fat from pan drippings. Combine cornstarch and ⅓ cup water, and add to pan drippings. Cook over medium heat, stirring constantly, until sauce is thickened. Season with salt and pepper to taste.

—*Dona J. Berge*
Dixon, Illinois

Sauerbraten Goose

1 medium boneless goose
1 cup red wine vinegar
1½ cups water
1 medium onion, sliced
2 bay leaves
5 whole cloves
3 teaspoons salt

2 celery stalks, cut into pieces
4 whole peppercorns or
  ¼ teaspoon pepper
2 tablespoons vegetable oil
2 tablespoons brown sugar
6 gingersnaps, crushed

Place goose in a glass bowl (do not use metal). Add vinegar and next 7 ingredients, stirring to coat goose. Cover and chill 1 to 2 days, turning goose frequently. Remove goose from marinade, reserving marinade. Brown goose in hot oil in a large Dutch oven. Reduce heat, and add 1½ cups reserved marinade. Simmer 2 hours or until goose is tender. Remove goose from Dutch oven, and place on a serving platter. Add sugar and gingersnap crumbs to pan drippings, and cook, stirring often, until thickened. Serve with wide egg noodles, red cabbage, mashed potatoes, or potato dumplings.

—*Aurora P. Stelz*
Falls Church, Virginia

Try this marinade with a venison rump roast. Whether using venison or goose, serve the savory sauerbraten with Merlot or other red wines.

97

Wildfowl Stroganoff

Beef Stroganoff
originated as a favorite
dish of the 19th century
Russian count of the
same name. Along with
adding goose, this
adaptation of the
classic calls for mirin,
which is a sweet
Japanese cooking wine.

½ goose breast fillet or 2 duck breast
    fillets, sliced across the grain
    into thin strips
1 tablespoon soy sauce
1 tablespoon mirin
¹⁄₁₆ teaspoon ground ginger
⅛ teaspoon black pepper
½ teaspoon sugar

6 to 12 dried shiitake mushrooms,
    soaked in warm water 15 minutes
4 tablespoons butter or margarine
1 medium onion, chopped
3 garlic cloves, minced
1 (10¾-ounce) can cream of
    mushroom soup, undiluted
½ to ¾ soup can of water
Hot cooked wild rice

Combine first 6 ingredients, stirring well, and chill 1 hour. Drain excess water from mushrooms, and slice into thin strips. Melt butter in a large skillet; add goose, onion, and garlic, and sauté until blood ceases to run. Add mushrooms, and sauté 3 to 5 minutes. Combine soup and water, and add to skillet. Cook until bubbling. Cover, reduce heat, and simmer 5 minutes. Serve over wild rice.

Yield: 4 servings

—*Lauren Aase*
Grand Forks AFB, North Dakota

Ginger Goose

½ teaspoon fresh slivered ginger
1 to 2 garlic cloves
¼ teaspoon dried red pepper flakes

2 tablespoons olive oil
1 (½-pound) goose breast, sliced
   across the grain into thin strips

Cook first 4 ingredients in a skillet over medium heat until garlic is tender. Add goose strips, and flash fry both sides just until done. Do not overcook. Serve immediately on crusty bread with cheese and red wine.

—*John Kubisiak*
Ashland, Missouri

Here's a meal for those who like spicy food. Ginger has a clean taste that feels warm on the tongue. This ginger goose can be prepared relatively quickly, and the leftovers make great sandwiches.

DU

Sweet-and-Sour Goose

Oriental sweet-and-sour is now a favorite staple in homes throughout North America. This recipe also works well with duck and other game.

2 goose breasts or 3 to 4 duck breasts,
    cubed (about 2 pounds)
2 cups water
½ cup apple juice
1 egg, lightly beaten
½ cup cornstarch
5 tablespoons vegetable oil
1 onion, cut into 1-inch pieces
3 carrots, sliced
1 garlic clove, pressed
2 tablespoons water

1 green bell pepper,
    cut into 1-inch pieces
1 tablespoon cornstarch
⅓ cup brown sugar
¼ teaspoon ground ginger
2 tablespoons soy sauce
¼ cup wine vinegar
¼ cup chicken broth
½ cup pineapple chunks
2 tomatoes

Combine first 3 ingredients in a glass bowl, and chill 3 hours. Remove goose from marinade, discarding marinade. Dip goose in egg, and dredge in cornstarch. Brown goose in 3 tablespoons hot oil in a large skillet. Remove goose, and set aside. Add remaining 2 tablespoons hot oil to skillet, and stir-fry onion, carrot, and garlic 1 minute. Add 2 tablespoons water and bell pepper. Cover and cook 2 minutes, stirring frequently. Combine cornstarch and brown sugar in a bowl. Add ginger and next 3 ingredients, stirring well. Return goose to skillet, and add pineapple, tomatoes, and cornstarch mixture. Cook 1 to 2 minutes or until thickened. Serve over steamed rice.

Yield: 4 to 6 servings.

—*Mark Anspach*
Ft. Collins, Colorado

Papa's Marinated Barbecue Goose

1 cup soy sauce
1 cup peanut or canola oil
1 tablespoon dried onion flakes
1 tablespoon dried parsley flakes
½ teaspoon minced garlic

1 teaspoon black pepper
2 tablespoons lemon juice
2 tablespoons red wine vinegar
  (optional)
Goose breast fillets

Combine first 7 ingredients, and optional vinegar, in a zip-top plastic bag; mix well. Add goose fillets, and chill 1 hour or overnight. Barbecue or bake according to desired method. Serve sliced very thin.

—Earl Dunnigan
Bismarck, North Dakota

Leftovers are delicious served on crackers with sharp Cheddar cheese. Papa's marinated Barbecue Goose is so good, however, you might not have any morsels left.

Royal Canadian Roast Goose

Instead of a glaze, the orange juice mixture can be served at the table as a sauce.

1 (6- to 8-pound) goose, dressed
Salt to taste
Oregano
1 cup chopped celery
1 cup chopped onion
1 garlic clove, minced
1 tablespoon olive oil
1½ to 2 apples, peeled and chopped
¼ cup chopped dried cranberries
¼ cup chopped dried apricot
2 tablespoons fresh chopped parsley
1 tablespoon dried sage
¼ teaspoon salt

¼ teaspoon pepper
½ teaspoon ground thyme
1 bay leaf, crumbled
1 egg
½ cup prune nectar or apple juice
3 cups coarse breadcrumbs
1 cup orange juice
½ cup chili sauce
1 tablespoon brown sugar
1 tablespoon soy sauce
1 teaspoon prepared mustard
¼ teaspoon garlic powder

Season goose inside and out with salt to taste and oregano. Sauté celery, onion, and garlic in hot oil in a skillet until tender. Transfer to a large bowl, and add apple and next 10 ingredients, stirring well. Add breadcrumbs until stuffing reaches desired consistency. Spoon stuffing into goose cavity. Cook orange juice and next 5 ingredients in a saucepan until bubbly. Cook 2 more minutes. Bake goose, breast side up, in a broiler pan at 350° for 3 hours to 3 hours and 30 minutes, covering with aluminum foil during last 30 minutes to prevent excessive browning and draining fat from pan as it accumulates. Brush orange glaze over goose during last 20 minutes of cooking. Serve with wild rice, green peas, salad, and red wine.

—*Murray G. Schultz*
Calgary, Alberta

102

Goose Pot Pie

1 (15-ounce) package refrigerated
   piecrusts
1 (10½-ounce) can condensed beef
   broth, undiluted
1 small potato, cut into ¼-inch cubes
   (optional)
½ small onion, chopped (optional)
1 celery stalk, chopped (optional)
½ cup fresh chopped mushrooms
   (optional)
1 (16-ounce) bag frozen mixed
   vegetables
4 wild goose or duck breasts

Salt and pepper to taste
Garlic powder to taste
2 to 3 tablespoons vegetable oil or
   bacon drippings
1 (10¾-ounce) can cream of
   mushroom soup, undiluted
2 to 3 tablespoons Worcestershire
   sauce
¼ teaspoon hot sauce
1 tablespoon browning-and-
   seasoning sauce
¼ cup red wine

For hungry crowds, make this recipe in large batches and freeze in zip-top bags. It tastes so good that you will never give away another goose.

Fit 1 piecrust into a 1½-quart baking dish, and bake according to package directions. Bring broth to a boil in a large saucepan, and add, if desired, potato, onion, celery and mushrooms; cook until tender. Add frozen vegetables, and boil 4 to 6 minutes. Reduce heat, and simmer. Season goose breasts with salt, pepper, and garlic to taste. Brown goose in hot oil in a skillet, leaving center rare. Remove breasts from skillet, and cut into small cubes. Add goose and pan drippings to vegetable mixture. Increase heat, and add mushroom soup, stirring until smooth. Add Worcestershire sauce and remaining ingredients, and cook 5 more minutes. Spoon mixture into prepared piecrust, and cover with the remaining piecrust. Crimp edges, and cut several small slits in top. Bake at 350° for 1 hour or until crust is golden brown. Let stand at room temperature 10 minutes before serving.

—Scott Lucy
Houston, Texas

DU

Harvest Roast Goose

Oven bags help lock in the moisture of the goose. To complete the taste, serve this tender goose with tart red cabbage and a hearty red wine or dark beer.

4 tablespoons butter or margarine
2 garlic cloves, minced
1 goose
Salt and pepper to taste

1 orange, quartered
1 apple, quartered
1 onion, quartered
1 cup apple cider

Melt 2 tablespoons butter in a skillet; add garlic, and sauté until tender. Rub garlic mixture on goose breast under loosened skin. Rub remaining 2 tablespoons butter over skin, legs, and cavity. Salt and pepper to taste. Place orange, apple, and onion in cavity. Bake goose in a roasting pan at 500° for 15 minutes. Remove from pan, and place in a large oven bag in roasting pan. Add cider. Reduce heat to 325*, and bake, covered, 2 hours and 30 minutes or until legs pull off easily.

—*Dave Wietecha*
Norfolk, Nebraska

Smoked Stuffed Waterfowl

1 goose or duck breast per person
1 (½-inch-thick) slice Monterey Jack
cheese with peppers per breast
1 tablespoon chopped green onion
per breast

1 (½-inch thick) slice tasso or smoked
ham per breast
Bacon slices
Barbecue or steak sauce

Soak goose in saltwater 24 hours to draw blood. Butterfly goose, and top each breast with cheese, green onion, and tasso. Roll up, jellyroll fashion, and wrap with several bacon slices; secure with wooden picks. Baste with barbecue sauce, and bake at 350° for 45 minutes to 1 hour, basting every 15 minutes with barbecue sauce. Serve with a green salad, rice, and red wine.

—*Mike Zimmermann*
Houston, Texas

Tabasco steak sauce gives this stuffed waterfowl a delicious zing. Barbecue sauce may be used, but offers a more mellow taste.

Dutch Oven Goose Drumsticks and Thighs

Here's a slow-cooking recipe perfect for tough goose portions. It's sure to turn them into tender delights.

4 skinless goose legs (drumsticks and thighs)
2 (10¾-ounce) cans condensed beef broth, undiluted
2 teaspoons minced garlic

2 tablespoons herbes de Provence
Pinch of coarsely ground pepper
1 onion, chopped
Cornstarch

Bring first 5 ingredients to a simmer in a Dutch oven. Transfer to oven, and bake, covered, at 275° for 2 hours. Add onion, and cook 1 more hour. Remove goose from Dutch oven, and remove meat from bones. Cut into small pieces. Add cornstarch to pan drippings to make gravy with desired consistency. Add goose meat, and simmer 15 minutes. Serve over rice, potatoes, or pasta.

—Robert E. Hill
Billings, Montana

Italian Goose

4 goose breasts
2 to 3 apples, cored
1 (4.5-ounce) can chopped
  green chiles

1 (1-ounce) envelope dry onion
  soup mix
Salt, pepper and garlic salt to taste

Cook goose and apple in a slow cooker 6 hours. Remove goose from slow cooker, and discard drippings. Shred goose, and return to slow cooker. Add green chiles and soup mix. Add water to desired consistency. Bring to a boil. Reduce heat, and simmer 2 hours. Add salt, pepper and garlic salt to taste.

—*Carl Gill*
Oakdale, Illinois

Canned chiles work better than fresh ones in this recipe due to their soft texture. If you prefer using fresh chile peppers, sauté them in olive oil to break down their firm exterior.

DU

Crock Pot Goose

Slow cookers turn tough goose into tender delights. This recipe combines sophisticated taste with the ease of slow cooking.

2 tablespoons butter or margarine
4 goose breasts
Salt and pepper to taste
2 celery stalks, sliced
½ red onion, chopped
1 garlic clove, chopped

2 shallots, chopped
1 (10½-ounce) can condensed
  chicken broth, undiluted
½ cup white wine
1 teaspoon dried thyme
1 bay leaf

Melt butter in a skillet; add goose, and sauté until browned. Transfer goose to a slow cooker, and add salt and pepper to taste. Sauté celery and next 3 ingredients in skillet until tender. Add broth and next 3 ingredients, and bring to a boil. Add celery mixture to slow cooker. Cook on LOW 6 to 8 hours. Remove goose to a serving platter. Pour drippings through a wire-mesh strainer into a nonstick skillet, and boil until reduced by half. Serve gravy with goose.

—*Lucinda Brown*
Milwaukie, Oregon

108

Smothered Goose

Flour
½ teaspoon salt
½ teaspoon pepper
2 goose breasts and legs,
   cut into bite-size pieces
1 stick butter or margarine

2 (8-ounce) containers sour cream
2 (10¾-ounce) cans cream of
   mushroom soup, undiluted
½ teaspoon soy sauce
½ teaspoon Worcestershire sauce
½ teaspoon paprika

Combine flour, salt, and pepper. Dredge goose in flour mixture. Melt butter in a skillet; add goose, and cook until browned. Remove goose from skillet, and pour off drippings, leaving a small portion. Add sour cream and next 4 ingredients, stirring well. Layer soup mixture and meat in a cast-iron Dutch oven, ending with soup mixture. Bake, covered, at 325° for 2 hours and 30 minutes. Serve over noodles or rice.

—*Matthew D. Hopkins*
Houston, Texas

Substitute any type of game meat for the goose. To reduce "gaminess," soak the meat in cold water and 1 tablespoon white vinegar.

Great Wild Goose Breast

Wild goose is naturally low in fat. To keep it as healthy as possible, use reduced-fat cream of chicken soup and chicken broth.

Butter or margarine
1 onion, chopped
Pancake mix
Salt and pepper to taste
Garlic salt
1 goose breast, cut into ¼-inch strips

1 (10¾-ounce) can cream of chicken
   soup, undiluted
1 (10½-ounce) can condensed
   chicken broth

Melt butter in a large skillet; add onion, and sauté until tender. Combine pancake mix, salt, pepper, and garlic salt to taste. Dredge goose in pancake mixture, and add to skillet. Cook until browned. Drain remaining butter from skillet, and add soup and broth. Simmer 1 hour and 30 minutes to 2 hours.

—Ralph Fischer
Pine City, Minnesota

110

Goose in the Bag

1 goose breast, cut into large pieces
1 large onion, sliced
4 potatoes, peeled and chopped
6 carrots, cut into pieces

¾ cup brown sugar
1½ cups water
Salt and pepper to taste

Combine all ingredients in a large oven bag, and place in a baking pan. Cut 6 slits in top of bag. Bake at 350° for 45 minutes to 1 hour, turning bag after 30 minutes. Serve with salad and fresh bread.

Yield: 4 servings.

—*Don Cholette, Jr.*
Wyandotte, Michigan

Oven bags make this meal easy to prepare. Serve the tender goose with salad, steamed vegetables, and fresh bread.

Louisiana Goose

1 goose or 2 ducks
1 package Tony's Creole Gumbo Mix
2 envelopes brown gravy mix

1 to 2 cups quick rice
Salt and pepper to taste

Bring goose and water to cover to a boil in a large Dutch oven. Boil until goose is done. Remove meat from bones, and return to goose stock. Add gumbo mix, gravy mix, and rice. Cook until rice is done.

Yield: 4 to 6 servings.

—*John Becton*
West Monroe, Louisiana

If Tony's Creole Gumbo Mix is not available in your area, use Zatarain's or other commercially packaged gumbo mixes.

UPLAND BIRDS

Delicate pheasant; succulent grouse; plump, tender dove—with recipes like these at your fingertips, who would ever have need of fast-food burgers again? Who would want to, with a variety like this from which to choose? From these pages, you can put together a feast as pleasing to the eye as to the palate, and one to rival the offerings of any four-star restaurant.

—*Billy Joe Cross*

Pheasant in a Fruit Wreath

Don't forget to top the pheasant with toasted pecans. To toast the nuts, place them on a baking sheet, and bake at 350° for 10 to 12 minutes.

4 pheasants, cut breasts and thighs into 1½-inch pieces
1 (14-ounce) can pineapple chunks
¼ cup brown sugar
½ teaspoon ground ginger
¼ teaspoon allspice
1 (6½-ounce) can frozen orange juice concentrate, thawed
½ cup chopped onion
¼ cup ketchup
¼ cup lemon juice
2 tablespoons soy sauce

1 garlic clove, minced
4 tablespoons cornstarch
⅓ cup fruit juice or water
1 (10-ounce) can Mandarin oranges, drained
1½ cups seedless green grapes
10 maraschino cherries
1 banana, cut into 1-inch diagonal slices
⅔ cup toasted whole pecans
Hot cooked wild rice

Place pheasant in a 13- x 9-inch baking dish. Drain pineapple chunks, reserving ½ cup juice and chunks. Combine ½ cup pineapple juice, brown sugar, and next 8 ingredients, stirring well. Pour over pheasant. Cover and chill several hours or overnight. Bake pheasant at 350° for 50 to 60 minutes or until tender, basting occasionally. Remove pheasant pieces to a warm serving platter. Cover and bake at 225° to keep warm. Combine cornstarch and fruit juice; add to drippings in baking dish. Bring to a boil, stirring constantly, until smooth and thick. Add additional cornstarch, if necessary, to reach desired consistency. Add reserved pineapple chunks, oranges, and next 3 ingredients. Cook over low heat, stirring often, until sauce bubbles and fruit is warm. Spoon fruit sauce around pheasant pieces on platter to resemble a wreath. Sprinkle with toasted pecans. Serve with rice.

Yield: 8 servings.

—Jim Powlesland
Calgary, Alberta

Roast Amber Apricot Pheasant

2 pheasants
Salt and pepper to taste
1 cup celery leaves
2 onion slices
2 lemon slices
2 small apples, halved
2 garlic cloves

6 bacon slices
2 cups chicken broth
1½ cups apricot jam
1 teaspoon lemon or orange rind
1 teaspoon cornstarch
2 teaspoons water

Season pheasants inside and out with salt and pepper, and place in a large ovenproof saucepan. Combine celery leaves and next 4 ingredients, and spoon mixture equally into pheasant cavities. Top each bird with 3 bacon slices. Bake at 350° for 30 minutes or until tender, basting occasionally. Remove pheasants to a serving platter; keep warm. Pour off fat from pan. Add chicken broth, and cook over medium heat until liquid is reduced by half, stirring to loosen browned particles. Add apricot jam, lemon rind, and salt and pepper to taste. Combine cornstarch and water; add to sauce. Reduce heat to low, and simmer 5 minutes or until sauce is thickened. Spoon sauce over birds and enjoy!

—Patricia P. Meyers
Edina, Minnesota

Apricot is a summer fruit, available between May and August. If they are in season, chop 2 or 3 of the rosy, yellow gems, and sprinkle them on top of the pheasant.

DU

115

Pheasant Marsala

You will be delighted with the rich, savory taste of the Marsala sauce. Instead of pheasant, try using other upland birds, such as partridge or quail.

2 medium boneless pheasant breasts, cubed
2 tablespoons oil
2 (8-ounce) packages fresh mushrooms, sliced
3 onions, chopped
2 garlic cloves, finely chopped

2 medium shallots, chopped
½ cup Marsala
1½ cups chicken broth (fat free and low sodium broth works well)
1 teaspoon balsamic vinegar
3 tablespoons all-purpose flour
Hot cooked egg noodles or rice

Brown pheasant cubes in hot oil in a large Dutch oven. Remove from pan. Add mushrooms to pan, and cook 7 minutes or until mushrooms give off liquid, adding additional oil if necessary to keep from sticking. Add onion, garlic, and shallots, and cook until browned. Add Marsala, and cook until thoroughly heated. Add chicken broth, and bring to a boil. Reduce heat, and simmer 15 minutes. Add balsamic vinegar, stirring well. Combine flour and 2 to 3 tablespoons gravy, stirring until flour is dissolved. Add flour mixture and pheasant to mushroom mixture, and simmer 5 minutes. Serve with egg noodles or rice.

—*Aurora P. Stelz*
Falls Church, Virginia

Pheasant in Mustard Sauce

2 boneless skinless pheasant breast
  halves
¼ teaspoon salt
⅛ teaspoon pepper
1 tablespoon butter or margarine
1 tablespoon vegetable oil
¼ cup chopped onion

1 garlic clove, minced
½ cup chicken broth
2 tablespoons lemon juice
3 tablespoons Dijon mustard
¾ teaspoon dried marjoram
Hot cooked rice

Sprinkle pheasant with salt and pepper. Melt butter in a large skillet; add oil and pheasant, and cook over medium heat 6 to 8 minutes or until browned. Combine onion and next 5 ingredients, and add to skillet. Bring to a boil; reduce heat, and simmer 15 to 20 minutes or until pheasant juices run clear. Serve over rice.

Yield: 2 servings.

—*Ingrid Spies*
Winona, Minnesota

Pheasant is both lean and delicate. To avoid drying out the meat, do not overcook. With this tasty mustard sauce, the pheasant is moist and delicious.

DU

Hot Skillet Pheasant

1 egg
1 cup milk
1 cup round buttery cracker crumbs
1 pheasant, cut into pieces

½ cup shortening
½ teaspoon salt
½ teaspoon pepper

Do not substitute saltine crackers for the crumb coating. Ritz crackers, or similar brands, offer a buttery taste and a warm caramel color.

Combine egg and ⅓ cup milk in a shallow dish, stirring well. Combine cracker crumbs, salt, and pepper in a separate dish. Dip pheasant in egg mixture, and dredge in crumb mixture. Brown pheasant in hot shortening in a heavy ovenproof skillet, turning occasionally. Add remaining ⅔ cup milk; cover and bake at 325° for 2 hours or until tender.

—Robert LaBuda
Berlin, Wisconsin

Classic Grilled Pheasant

2 boneless pheasant breasts, cut into
   1-x 3-inch strips
Lemon pepper to taste
Salt to taste
½ bacon slice
1 tablespoon butter or margarine

½ medium onion, chopped
1 celery stalk, chopped
½ green bell pepper, chopped
2 tablespoons frozen orange juice
   concentrate or clam juice

This recipe is easy and delicious with no dishes to clean. You can even prepare it around an open campfire.

Combine all ingredients in an aluminum foil pot, sealing top. Grill over medium heat (300° to 350°) 15 minutes. Serve directly from aluminum foil.

—*J. M. Freimuth*
Palos Heights, Illinois

DU

Pheasant in Sour Cream

Since wild pheasant is naturally lean, gear your meal to the healthy side. Use nonfat sour cream and low-fat milk.

1 pheasant, cut into pieces
Salt and pepper to taste
Flour
½ cup vegetable oil
1½ (8-ounce) containers sour cream
½ cup milk

Season pheasant with salt and pepper, and dust with flour. Brown pheasant in hot oil. Remove pheasant and drippings to a baking pan. Combine sour cream and milk, and pour over pheasant. Cover and bake at 325° for 1 hour to 1 hour and 15 minutes or until tender.

Yield: 2 to 4 servings.

—*Mary Nichols*
Helena, Montana

Tender Mushroom Pheasant

1 or 2 Pheasant
Pickling salt
¼ cup chopped onion
1 (10¾-ounce) can cream of
   mushroom soup, undiluted

1 (10¾-ounce) can cream of chicken
   soup, undiluted
1 soup can of water
1 (4-ounce) can mushrooms, drained
½ teaspoon peppercorns

Soak pheasant in pickling salt for 1 to 2 hours. Cut off legs at backbone, and split. Place in a slow cooker. Add onion and remaining ingredients. Cook on LOW 4 hours or until tender.

Yield: 4 servings.

—*Richard Tulius*
Rochester, Minnesota

For tender pheasant, this dish is sure to hit the spot. The rich sauce may be used as gravy, so don't forget the potatoes or rice. Crusty bread is a must to sop up the tasty sauce.

Garlic Roast Pheasant

When purchasing garlic,
buy fresh bulbs that are
sold individually. Avoid
garlic that is discolored
or sprouting.

1 (2 to 3-pound) pheasant, dressed
Salt and pepper to taste
1 lemon slice
1 bay leaf
1 garlic clove, minced
3 to 6 celery leaves

4 bacon slices
Melted butter or margarine
1 large onion, sliced
2 (4-ounce) cans mushrooms
1 cup chicken broth

Sprinkle pheasant with salt and pepper inside and out, and place in a baking pan. Place lemon and next 3 ingredients in cavity. Truss pheasant, and top breast with bacon. Cover pheasant with cheesecloth soaked in melted butter. Arrange onion and mushrooms around pheasant. Add broth. Bake at 350° for 30 minutes per pound or until tender. Remove cloth and bay leaf, and discard.

—Jim Jares
Laramie, Wyoming

122

Game Bird Casserole

½ pound uncooked elbow macaroni
  or seashell pasta
2 to 4 tablespoons butter or
  margarine
1 onion, chopped
2 celery stalks, chopped
2 (8-ounce) packages fresh
  mushrooms, sliced

3 carrots, chopped
1 sweet potato, sliced
Salt and pepper to taste
1 (10¾-ounce) can golden
  mushroom soup, undiluted
2 soup cans of water
2 pheasant breasts, cut up

Combine pasta and next 7 ingredients in a 2-quart baking dish. Add soup and water, stirring well. Add pheasant; cover and bake at 350° for 40 minutes or until pasta is tender.

—*Aurora Stelz*
Falls Church, Virginia

Casseroles are traditionally easy meals to prepare because only 1 baking dish is used. In this recipe, even the pasta cooks in the casserole.

Pheasant-Potato Bake

If you don't care for green bell pepper, feel free to substitute broccoli or other vegetables.

3 to 6 boneless skinless pheasant
  breasts
Schilling broiled steak seasoning
6 to 8 cups thinly sliced unpeeled
  new potato
1 medium onion, thinly sliced
1 medium green bell pepper, thinly
  sliced
1 (4-ounce) can mushrooms

2 (10¾-ounce) cans cream of
  mushroom soup, undiluted
1 tablespoon chicken bouillon
  granules
1 cup cubed process cheese spread
  loaf
1 tablespoon dried parsley flakes
¼ teaspoon minced garlic
Salt and pepper to taste

Season pheasant breasts on both sides with Schilling seasoning. Brown pheasant in a large heavy skillet. Remove from pan to a 13- x 9-inch baking dish. Place potato in a large bowl, and fill halfway with water. Microwave at HIGH until potato is tender. Sauté onion, mushrooms, and bell pepper in skillet until tender; layer over pheasant. Combine soup, next 5 ingredients, and 1½ cups water from cooked potato in a large bowl. Top chicken with potato, and add soup mixture. Bake at 325° for 30 minutes.

—*Earl J. Dunnigan*
Bismarck, North Dakota

Pheasant Paprika

1 pheasant, skinned
Flour
Pepper
Olive oil
1 medium onion, diced
4 to 5 garlic cloves, minced
½ green bell pepper, diced
2 large tomatoes, quartered
1 cup sliced mushrooms

2 cups pheasant or chicken broth
1 bay leaf
½ teaspoon ground oregano
½ teaspoon ground thyme
2 tablespoons hot Hungarian
  paprika
1 jalapeño pepper, seeded and diced
  (optional)
1 cup wine (optional)

Cut pheasant into serving-size pieces, reserving the back and breastbones to make pheasant broth, if desired. Dredge pheasant in flour and pepper, and brown in hot oil in a cast-iron Dutch oven. Remove pheasant, and set aside. Sauté onion and garlic in hot oil until tender, adding more oil if necessary. Add bell pepper, tomato, and mushrooms, and cook until vegetables are browned. Add broth, next 4 ingredients, and, if desired, jalapeño and wine. Add browned pheasant to mixture, and simmer 1½ hours, stirring every 10 minutes. Remove bay leaf, and discard. Serve with mashed potatoes, rice, or pasta.

Yield: 2 to 3 servings.

—*Paul F. Vang*
Butte, Montana

For a less spicy version of this meal, omit the jalapeño and substitute sweet paprika for the hot Hungarian paprika. Consider serving this rich, savory dish with a glass of Cabernet Sauvignon or Zinfandel.

DU

Pheasant Squares

To serve, spoon the rich sauce over each square. You'll find this meal both delicious and filling.

1 (8-ounce) package stuffing mix
½ cup butter or margarine, melted
1 cup chicken broth
2½ cups cooked cubed pheasant
½ cup chopped onion
½ cup finely chopped celery
½ cup Miracle Whip
¾ teaspoon salt
2 eggs
1½ cups milk

1 (10¾-ounce) can cream of
  mushroom soup, undiluted
1 cup (4 ounces) shredded Cheddar
  cheese
½ (10¾-ounce) can cream of
  mushroom soup, undiluted
2 tablespoons milk
½ cup sour cream
⅓ cup chopped pimento-stuffed
  olives

Combine first 3 ingredients in a 13- x 9-inch baking dish. Combine pheasant and next 6 ingredients, and spread evenly over stuffing mixture. Cover and chill at least 6 hours. Uncover, and add 1 can soup. Bake at 325° for 40 minutes. Sprinkle with Cheddar cheese, and bake 10 more minutes. Cool and cut into squares. Cook ½ can soup and next 3 ingredients in a small saucepan until thoroughly heated.

Yield: 9 to 12 servings.

—*Patricia Olson*
Ipswich, South Dakota

126

Pheasant Stew with Hot Bean Sauce

1 tablespoon vegetable oil
2 dashes garlic powder
1 pheasant, cut into 1-inch cubes
1 teaspoon sugar
2 tablespoons hot bean sauce
½ cup water (optional)

Basil
Celery leaves (optional)
Salt to taste
Potatoes
Carrots

Cook oil and garlic powder in a large saucepan over medium to medium-high heat until garlic powder is browned. Add pheasant, and cook, stirring slowly. Add sugar, and cook until pheasant is browned, stirring slowly. Add bean sauce, and cook, stirring slowly. Add ½ cup of water, if needed to reach desired consistency. Add basil and, if desired, celery leaves, and cook 3 minutes or until meat is done. Add water to just below the meat level. Cover and bring to a boil. Add salt to taste. Cover, reduce heat, and simmer 30 to 60 minutes. Add potatoes and carrots, and bring to a boil. Reduce heat, and simmer until vegetables are tender.

—*Mark Alpher*
Grand Haven, Michigan

If you like spicy food, increase the amount of bean sauce and reduce the salt. Hot bean sauce is often found in the International section of supermarkets. If you can't find it in your market, look for the sauce in a Vietnamese specialty shop.

127

Uncle Todd's Pheasant Under Glass

Here's a down-home
version of pheasant
under glass. In this
case, the glass is the
slow cooker lid.

1 (10¾-ounce) can cream of
  mushroom soup, undiluted
1 (10¾-ounce) can cream of chicken
  soup, undiluted
1 (1-ounce) envelope dry onion
  soup mix

1 (4-ounce) can mushroom stems
  and pieces
2 celery stalks, chopped
1½ cups quick-cooking rice
1½ cups water
¼ cup soy sauce
1 large pheasant, cut up

Combine mushroom soup and next 7 ingredients in a slow cooker; sink pheasant pieces to the bottom. Cover and cook on LOW 8 to 10 hours.

Yield: 5 servings or enough for 1 hungry teenager.

—*Todd Brumm*
Reeseville, Wisconsin

Onion Ring-Necked Pheasant

Pheasant breasts and thighs,
    cut into pieces
Flour
Pepper
Vegetable oil

Sour cream
1 (10¾-ounce) can cream of
    mushroom soup
¼ to ½ cup mushrooms
1 can French fried onions

Dredge pheasant in flour and pepper, and brown in hot oil in a large skillet. Remove pheasant to a 13- x 9-inch baking dish, and cover with sour cream. Add soup and mushrooms, and bake at 325° for 30 minutes. Top with fried onions, and bake 10 to 15 more minutes.

—Fraser Kulba
Winnipeg, Manitoba

Whether you serve the pheasant over noodles or mashed potatoes, you are sure to enjoy the delicate-flavored meat and hearty, cream sauce.

DU

Fort Randall Pheasant

To fully enjoy every drop of the creamy sauce, serve this rich, delicious meal with crusty French bread.

3 boneless pheasant breasts, cut into serving pieces
Milk
1 tablespoon paprika
2 cups biscuit mix
½ teaspoon cumin
2 tablespoons basil
Vegetable oil
4 potatoes, cut into large pieces

1 (8-ounce) package sliced fresh mushrooms
1 large onion, diced
3 carrots, cut into large pieces
1 (10¾-ounce) can cream of chicken soup, undiluted
1 (10¾-ounce) can cream of mushroom soup, undiluted
2 soup cans of water

Soak pheasant in milk overnight in the refrigerator. Combine biscuit mix, paprika, cumin, and 1 tablespoon basil. Dredge pheasant in paprika mixture. Pour oil to a depth of 3-inches in a large Dutch oven; heat to 375°. Fry pheasant in hot oil until browned. Drain on paper towels. Arrange pheasant, potato, and next 3 ingredients in a 2-quart baking dish. Combine soups and 2 cans water, and add to pheasant mixture. Add remaining 1 tablespoon basil. Bake, covered, at 350° for 1 hour. Uncover and bake 30 more minutes.

Yield: 6 servings.

—*Donna Tonelli*
Lake Andes, South Dakota

Pheasant with Ginger, Scallion, and Garlic

1 large or 2 small pheasant, cut into
    pieces
Salt and pepper to taste
2 tablespoons soy sauce
2 tablespoons olive oil
4 garlic cloves, minced
3 tablespoons dry sherry

1 teaspoon grated fresh ginger
2 tablespoons honey
3 scallions, thinly sliced
2 cups heavy whipping cream
2 tablespoons soy sauce
¼ cup Dijon mustard

Season pheasant with salt and pepper, and place in a large (14- x 20-inch) oven bag. Place oven bag in a 2-inch-deep roasting pan. Whisk together soy sauce and next 5 ingredients. Add soy sauce mixture to oven bag; close bag with twist tie, and marinate 1 hour. Open bag, and add scallions. Close bag, and make 6 (½-inch) slits in top. Bake at 375° for 45 minutes to 1 hour or until juices run clear when legs are pierced.

—Glenn Davis
Gwynedd, Pennsylvania

Use the drippings from the bag as a sauce. To serve, spoon the sauce onto warmed plates, and place the pheasant on top. You may substitute 3 grouse, halved, for pheasant. Cook grouse 45 minutes or less.

DU

Snipe Supreme

8 to 10 snipe
3 tablespoons butter or margarine
½ onion, finely chopped
2 garlic cloves, chopped

3 tablespoons olive oil
4 tablespoons Marsala
Hot cooked rice

Marsala adds a rich, sweet flavor to the delicate snipe. Inexpensive Marsala works well for cooking. Serve finer Marsala as a dessert wine.

Hang snipe securely. Skin snipe, and remove legs, breast fillets, and wishbone meat. Melt butter in a skillet; add onion, garlic, and oil, and sauté until tender. Add snipe pieces, and sauté over medium-high heat 6 to 8 minutes, turning once. Add Marsala; reduce heat, and simmer 2 to 3 minutes. Serve immediately with rice.

—Gary Lease
Santa Cruz, California

Fried Chukar

1 to 2 cups flour
½ teaspoon salt
½ to 1 teaspoon pepper
½ tablespoon Schillings Season-all
1 chukar, cut into pieces

3 to 4 tablespoons vegetable oil
1 to 2 cups water
¼ cup flour
4 to 6 cups milk

Combine first 4 ingredients in a shallow dish. Dredge chukar in flour mixture, and fry in hot oil in a heavy skillet over medium-high heat until browned, turning occasionally. Add 1 to 2 cups water; cover, reduce heat, and simmer 30 minutes or until meat is no longer pink and is tender. Remove chukar from skillet, and place on a serving platter. Add ¼ cup flour and milk to pan drippings, and cook until thickened, whisking constantly.

—*Jenny Christensen*
Bear River City, Utah

Chukar is a type of partridge from Asia and the Near East. While true partridges are not native to North America, they have been introduced as game birds as well as raised on farms.

Ptarmigan or Grouse in Rice

Ptarmigan may be found throughout mountain terrain and northern climates. This grouse possesses unique feathered feet. If it is not available, other grouse or upland birds may be substituted.

2 ptarmigan or grouse, cut into
  pieces
Krusteas Fry Mix
2 tablespoons olive oil
2 to 3 garlic cloves, sliced
Ground red pepper
Poultry seasoning

Salt-free herb-and-spice blend
1 (10¾-ounce) can cream of
  mushroom or chicken soup,
  undiluted
2 soup cans of water
1 cup rice

Dredge ptarmigan in fry mix, and brown in hot oil in an ovenproof skillet. Remove ptarmigan from skillet. Sprinkle garlic and next 3 ingredients to taste over ptarmigan. Add soup and water to skillet, and cook, stirring to loosen browned particles. Add rice, stirring well. Add seasoned ptarmigan, and cover. Bake at 325° for 2 hours and 30 minutes. Add additional milk or water to keep moist, if necessary.

—Sanna G. LeVan
Seward, Alaska

Chow Mein Grouse

2 grouse fillets
Olive oil
1 small onion, chopped
1 (8-ounce) package fresh
    mushrooms

3 tablespoons brown sauce
3 tablespoons soy sauce
2 cans chow mein vegetables
1⅓ cups cooked rice
Chow mein noodles

Stir-fry grouse in hot oil in a skillet until desired degree of doneness. Remove meat from skillet, and place in a 5-quart pan. Add water to a depth of 3 inches. Add onion and next 3 ingredients, and cook 30 minutes. Add chow mein vegetables, and cook 10 more minutes. Serve with rice and chow mein noodles.

Yield: 3 to 4 servings.

—*Chuck Kartak*
Center City, Minnesota

Here's a delicious and versatile waterfowl recipe. Feel free to substitute 1 pheasant or 2 puddle ducks for grouse.

Grouse or Sage Hen Kahlua Stir-fry

Kahlua offers deep, rich flavor to this stir-fry. If you do not wish to cook with alcohol, substitute 1 tablespoon cream and 2 tablespoons coffee.

1 egg
¼ cup vegetable oil
1 teaspoon cornstarch
1 to 2 pounds boneless skinless grouse or sage hen, cut into ½-inch strips
6 asparagus tips, fresh or canned
1 green bell pepper, cut into thin strips
1 (4-ounce) can sliced mushrooms
1 (4-ounce) can snow pea pods
½ cup chestnuts, sliced
3 tablespoons Kahlua
1 cup cashews
Hot cooked rice
Garnish: 3 green onions, chopped

Combine egg, 2 tablespoons oil, and ½ teaspoon cornstarch. Dredge grouse in egg mixture. Brown grouse in remaining 2 tablespoons hot oil in a large skillet. Drain well, reserving 2 tablespoons drippings in skillet. Remove grouse from skillet. Add asparagus and next 4 ingredients to skillet; stir-fry 3 minutes. Combine Kahlua and ½ teaspoon cornstarch, and add to skillet. Bring to a boil; reduce heat, and simmer until slightly thickened. Add grouse and cashews, and cook until thoroughly heated. Remove to a serving platter. Serve with rice. Garnish, if desired.

—*Elizabeth Rinn*
Jackson, Wyoming

A "Three-in-One" Bird

1 (10- to 12-pound) boneless capon,
  with legs and skin intact
Salt and freshly ground pepper
  to taste
Poultry seasoning and ground herbs
1 cup lingonberry or cranberry sauce
  (optional)

1 (5- to 7-pound) boneless skinless
  pheasant
2 boneless skinless chukar
Olive oil
4 to 6 bacon slices (optional)
Flour

Place capon, skin side down, on a flat surface. Season with salt, pepper, and poultry seasoning to taste. Spread with a thin layer of lingonberry sauce, if desired. Place the pheasant flat on the capon. Season the pheasant with salt, pepper, and poultry seasoning to taste. Repeat procedure with chukar. Roll the 3 layers of meat into the shape of a bird, and tie with string. Place the bird, breast side up, on a rack in a roasting pan. Rub the skin with olive oil, and place bacon over bird breast, if desired. Place the bird in a preheated 450° oven. Immediately reduce heat to 325°, and bake 5 to 6 hours or until meat thermometer placed in thickest portion of meat registers 180°, basting frequently. Remove bird to a serving platter, and cover with aluminum foil. Let stand at room temperature 15 to 20 minutes before serving. Remove grease from roasting pan, and add flour and water to make gravy. Serve with remaining lingonberry sauce and gravy.

—Len Ugarenko
Silver Spring, Maryland

Substitute 2 quail, 2 pigeon, or 2 small grouse for chukar, if desired. Anyway you prepare it, the leftovers are great, hot or cold.

Wild Turkey

1 (18- to 23-pound) wild turkey
Salad dressing
Apples
Onion

Oranges
Poultry seasoning
Paprika

Although wild turkey takes a long time to cook, seasoning and stuffing the bird is rather simple.

Coat outside of turkey with salad dressing. Fill cavity with apples, onion, and oranges. Season with poultry seasoning, and sprinkle with paprika. Place turkey in a roasting bag, and bake at 250° for 7 to 8 hours.

—*Sandi Beitzel*
Manitowoc, Wisconsin

138

Savory Turkey

1 turkey (1 pound per person)
1 orange, halved
Favorite stuffing
2 large carrots, quartered
2 celery stalks, halved

1 large onion, quartered
⅔ cup water or stock
1 stick butter or margarine, melted
½ cup tawny port

Rub inside and outside of turkey with orange halves. Fill with stuffing in neck and body. Close vents, and truss bird. Place carrot, celery, and onion in the bottom of a broiler pan. Add ⅔ cup water. Bake at 350° for 12 to 15 minutes per pound, basting with melted butter every 45 minutes. In last 45 minutes, baste with port every 15 minutes. Let stand at room temperature 15 minutes before serving.

—Karl Kaiser
Scottsdale, Arizona

This savory bird produces flavorful drippings. Pour them through a wire-mesh strainer into a saucepan. Bring to a boil; reduce heat, and slowly add a mixture of ¼ cup flour and water. Season with salt and pepper, and you have a delicious gravy.

DU

Bruised Buzzard Wings

Do not substitute chicken wings for turkey wings. They would fall apart and turn into "Bashed Budgie Wings."

Enough turkey wings to fill large roasting pan
1 cup soy sauce
1 cup honey

2 garlic cloves, minced or 1 teaspoon garlic salt
1 teaspoon seasoned salt
1 teaspoon Greek seasoning
2 tablespoons ketchup

Bake turkey wings at 350° for 2 hours to 2 hours and 30 minutes, basting and turning every 15 minutes. Combine soy sauce and next 5 ingredients. Serve turkey wings with sauce.

- *For extra-hot buzzard wings sauce, omit soy sauce and honey. Add 1 cup water, ½ cup hot sauce, ½ cup garlic or onion barbecue sauce, ½ cup brown sugar, and a dash of liquid smoke.*

—Kim Black
Aylmer, Ontario

140

Baja Deep-Fried Quail Breast

3 cups flour
Salt and red pepper to taste
½ teaspoon garlic powder
1 teaspoon onion powder

¼ teaspoon ground coriander
1 dozen quail breasts
Peanut oil
1 lime, halved

Combine first 5 ingredients in a shallow dish; dredge quail in flour mixture. Pour oil to a depth of 2 inches into a Dutch oven; heat to 350°. Fry quail until they float to the top. Squeeze lime juice over quail.

—Gary Caddell
Chula Vista, California

Serve this hot dish with an ice cold beer or beverage of your choice. For a new drink sensation, see the beverage recipes listed in this cookbook.

DU

Greek Quail

If fresh herbs are available, substitute them for dried. One tablespoon fresh herbs equals ½ teaspoon dried crushed or ¼ teaspoon ground.

½ cup olive oil
⅓ cup lemon juice
6 garlic cloves, minced
½ teaspoon dried crushed thyme

¼ teaspoon salt
¼ teaspoon ground pepper
½ teaspoon dried crushed oregano
12 quail, breasts and drumsticks

Combine first 7 ingredients in a shallow dish, stirring well. Wash quail, and pat dry. Add quail to marinade, and chill 1 hour or overnight. Grill quail over high heat (400° to 450°) 3 to 5 minutes on each side or until browned and tender. Beware of coals flaring.

Yield: 4 servings.

—*David M. Brown*
Plano, Texas

Easy Baked Quail

6 to 10 quail
Salt to taste
Butter or margarine
Flour
¼ cup water

3 tablespoons butter or margarine,
  melted
½ cup cooking sherry
¼ teaspoon marjoram

Season quail with salt to taste. Place 1 teaspoon butter in each quail cavity. Rub quail with butter, and dust lightly with flour. Place quail in a 13- x 9-inch baking dish. Combine ¼ cup water and next 3 ingredients, stirring well. Bake quail at 275° for 1 hour, basting often with sauce.

—*Quince L. Mitchell*
Corpus Christi, Texas

For a richer sauce, use Madeira instead of sherry. This sweet, dark wine is more expensive but adds a fuller flavor. If using Madeira, reduce the amount by half.

DU

Hearty Browned Quail

8 quail breasts
8 bacon slices
1 (6.2-ounce) package long-grain and
   wild rice mix
1 envelope Knorr Hunter sauce mix

½ cup minced onion
½ cup sliced mushrooms
½ cup diced potato
Salt and pepper to taste

In parts of the South, quail is called partridge but is more widely known as bobwhite. To determine serving sizes, calculate 2 to 3 birds per person.

Wrap quail breasts in bacon, and secure with wooden picks. Prepare rice and sauce mix according to package directions, and place in a baking dish; add onion, mushrooms, potato, and salt and pepper to taste. Place quail breasts on top of rice mix. Bake at 400° for 40 minutes or until liquid is absorbed, turning after 20 minutes. Brown under oven broiler just before serving.

—*Duran Shaves*
Shelbyville, Tennessee

144

Sour Cream-Dove Enchiladas

2 (10¾-ounce) cans cream of chicken
 soup, undiluted
½ cup sour cream
1 (4.5-ounce) can diced green chiles
½ teaspoon salt
10 cooked cubed dove breasts
2 cups (8 ounces) grated cheese

½ cup chopped onion
1 (8-ounce) package cream cheese,
 softened
2 tablespoons milk
1 dozen corn tortillas
Vegetable oil

Cook first 4 ingredients in a small saucepan until thoroughly heated. Do not boil. Combine dove and next 4 ingredients in a bowl. Dip tortillas in hot oil to soften. Fill tortillas evenly with dove mixture, and roll up, jellyroll fashion. Place, seam side down, in a 9- x 13-inch baking dish. Cover with sauce. Bake at 350° for 30 minutes.

—*Cheralynn A. Schnepp*
Tucson, Arizona

Green chiles give this creamy sauce a kick. Canned chiles work quite well due to their soft texture. If using fresh chile peppers, dice them, and sauté in olive oil to break down their firmness.

Sharon's Grilled Dove Breast

To prevent the delicate dove breasts from sticking, brush the cold grill with oil or spray it with nonstick coating. Do this before the grill is hot to avoid flare-ups.

24 dove breasts
½ cup baking soda
¾ teaspoon salt

Fat-free Italian dressing
Creole seasoning
Garlic pepper

Place dove in a large bowl, and cover with water. Add baking soda and salt. Cover and chill 2 to 4 hours, stirring once or twice. Remove dove from marinade, discarding marinade; rinse. Return dove to bowl, and add Italian dressing, Creole seasoning, and garlic pepper, stirring to mix. Cover, and chill 2 to 4 hours, stirring once or twice. Grill breasts, bone side down, over medium heat (300° to 350°) 20 minutes, turning last few minutes to brown sides. Baste during cooking with fresh Italian dressing (add beer to Italian dressing, if desired). Do not overcook.

—Larry Locke
Bryan, Texas

Dove Breast Hot Shots

Dove breasts, filleted (as many as you like)
1 jar sliced jalapeño peppers

1 (8-ounce) package Monterey Jack cheese, cut into small pieces
Bacon slices (1 slice for each breast)
Meat marinade of your choice

Wrap 2 fillets, 2 jalapeño pepper slices, and 2 pieces of cheese inside 1 bacon slice; secure with a wooden pick. Place in a shallow dish; add marinade, and chill at least 2 hours. Grill according to desired method.

—Kevin Church
Glenpool, Oklahoma

Be careful not to place the meat too close to the coals. Bacon drippings will flare up and char the meat.

Island Farm Dove

Rice and potatoes are natural side dishes with this creamy sauce and pan-fried dove. A mixed green salad, steamed vegetables, and hot French bread round out the meal.

12 boneless dove breasts
Salt and pepper to taste
2 onions, chopped
6 bacon slices
2 cups beer
1 (10¾-ounce) can cream of celery
   soup, undiluted

1 (10¾-ounce) can cream of
   mushroom soup, undiluted
1 (4-ounce) can mushrooms
2 tablespoons dried parsley flakes
½ lemon, sliced

Season dove with salt and pepper to taste. Brown dove in a skillet; remove dove from skillet. Sauté onion and bacon in skillet until onion is transparent. Combine dove, onion, bacon, beer, and soups in a 13- x 9-inch baking dish, stirring well. Top with mushrooms, parsley flakes, and lemon. Bake at 325° for 2 hours or until tender.

Yield: 4 servings.

—Raymond Ruth
Richmond, Virginia

148

Oven-Braised Doves

12 doves
Salt and pepper to taste
6 tablespoons butter or margarine
3 tablespoons flour
2 cups chicken broth

½ cup sherry
2 (4-ounce) cans mushrooms
½ cup parsley, minced
Hot cooked rice

Season doves with salt and pepper to taste. Melt butter in a heavy skillet; brown doves. Remove doves from skillet, and place in a 2-quart baking dish. Add flour to skillet, stirring well. Gradually add broth and sherry. Salt and pepper to taste, stirring well. Pour sauce over doves. Add mushrooms and parsley. Bake, covered, at 350° for 1 hour. Serve with rice.

—*Cindy Harper*
Humboldt, Tennessee

These tiny birds are quite lean and should not be overcooked. Heat the dove in a skillet just enough to brown the outside. They will be fully cooked after baking in the savory sauce for 1 hour.

DU

Pot-Roasted Mourning Doves

To enhance the down-home taste of this meal, serve black-eyed peas, greens, and fresh bread.

3 large yellow onions
1 large bell pepper
3 celery stalks
1 pound pork sausage
24 doves (do not pop out breast)
1 pound smoked sausage, sliced
Red pepper, black pepper, salt, and
  garlic powder to taste

1 garlic clove
1 stick butter or margarine
2 cans chicken broth
2 large cans sliced mushrooms,
  drained
1 bunch green onion tops, chopped

Finely chop 1 onion, ⅓ bell pepper, and 1½ celery stalks; combine chopped vegetables and pork sausage, and place inside each dove cavity. Place 1 smoked sausage slice over stuffing, and secure with a wooden pick. Season dove to taste. Finely chop remaining 2 onions, ⅔ bell pepper, and 1½ celery stalks, and place in a large Dutch oven. Add garlic and 2 tablespoons butter, and sauté over medium heat 20 to 30 minutes or until tender. Remove from Dutch oven, and set aside. Brown dove, 4 or 5 at a time, in remaining butter in Dutch oven, turning often. Remove dove from Dutch oven, and set aside. Drain excess grease. Return vegetables to Dutch oven, and add ½ can broth. Cook vegetables until desired degree of doneness. Return dove to Dutch oven, and add remaining 1½ cans broth. Cover and simmer 1 hour to 1 hour and 30 minutes or until dove is tender. Add mushrooms and chopped onion approximately 30 minutes before serving.

Yield: 6 to 8 servings.

—*Ed Villien*
Lafayette, Louisiana

WILD GAME

The most finicky eaters will be unable to say no to platters of savory deer, moose, elk, or antelope venison. Even those who may think they don't like wild game such as squirrel, rabbit, and turtle will be pleasantly surprised how tender and flavorful they are when prepared correctly, while those of us who already know will be too busy eating to laugh.

—*Billy Joe Cross*

Hunter's Venison Pie

Feel free to add additional vegetables to this pie. This is a delicious way to clean out your refrigerator.

1 large onion, diced
1 tablespoon vegetable oil
3 garlic cloves, minced
1 (1½- to 2-pound) venison roast,
    cut into bite-size pieces
1 (28-ounce) can tomatoes, drained
    and quartered
1 bay leaf
1 cup beer
Salt and pepper to taste

1 (8-ounce) package frozen peas,
    thawed
6 carrots, sliced
1 cup flour
¾ cup cornmeal
1 tablespoon sugar
½ teaspoon salt
1 cup milk
1 egg
3 tablespoons butter or margarine

Sauté onion in hot oil in a skillet until tender; add garlic, and sauté 1 minute (do not brown garlic). Add venison, and sauté until browned. Add tomatoes and next 3 ingredients, and simmer 1 hour or until meat is tender. Add peas and carrot, and simmer 15 minutes. Remove bay leaf, and discard. Combine flour and next 3 ingredients; add milk, egg, and butter, stirring until moistened. Transfer venison mixture into a baking dish; top with cornmeal batter. Bake at 425° for 25 to 30 minutes or until crust is browned.

Yield: 6 servings.

—Joan Miller
Lithonia, Georgia

Smoked Venison Ham Roast

4 cups white vinegar
1 (10- to 15-ounce) can tomato sauce
  or paste
1 (12-ounce) can beer
  (homemade preferred)
½ cup molasses
¼ cup extra-virgin olive oil
1 tablespoon salt

1 tablespoon dried basil
1 tablespoon lemon pepper
1 tablespoon paprika
1 tablespoon crushed red pepper
Pinch of garlic salt
Venison Ham
Bacon slices, chopped
2 quarts cranberry juice

Bring first 11 ingredients to a boil in a large saucepan. Reduce heat, and simmer 30 minutes, stirring occasionally. Remove from heat, and cool. Place venison in a large roasting pan, and add marinade. Chill 2 days, turning daily. Remove venison from marinade, discarding marinade. Secure bacon pieces around venison using wooden picks. Prepare charcoal fire in smoker, and let burn 15 to 20 minutes. Place water pan in smoker, and add cranberry juice; add water to depth of fill line. Place venison on food rack, and cook 4 to 6 hours or until meat thermometer inserted in thickest portion registers 170°.

—Oswell McLamb
Carrboro, North Carolina

The originator of this recipe perfected it through endless trials on rainy days. A delicious meal has been developed. It even won a ribbon in the WLA Wild Game Cook-off contest.

DU

Barbecued Venison Roast

Roast venison until medium rare. This enhances the full, rich flavor of the meat. To spice it up, add a little hot pepper to season the sauce.

1 venison roast
2 tablespoons brown sugar
1 cup chopped onion
1 cup chopped celery
1 cup ketchup
1 cup water
¼ cup vinegar
Desired seasonings

Cook venison according to desired method until tender. Let cool; slice into thin pieces, and place in a 13- x 9-inch baking dish. Simmer brown sugar and next 6 ingredients in a large saucepan until thoroughly heated. Pour sauce over venison, and bake at 350° for 1 hour. Serve on buns.

—*Arlene Naber*
Plymouth, Wisconsin

Venison-Carrot Casserole

1 teaspoon butter or margarine
1 pound ground venison
¼ cup minced onion
4 garlic cloves, minced
2 (8-ounce) cans tomato sauce
1 teaspoon salt
¼ teaspoon pepper

1 cup sour cream
1 cup creamy cottage cheese
Chopped fresh parsley
1 cup sliced cooked carrots
8 ounces medium noodles, cooked
1 cup (4 ounces) shredded Cheddar
  cheese

Melt butter in a skillet; add venison, onion, and garlic, and cook until meat is browned. Add tomato sauce, salt, and pepper, and simmer 5 minutes. Combine sour cream and next 3 ingredients in a large bowl; add noodles, stirring well. Layer noodle mixture and venison mixture in a lightly greased 3-quart baking dish, beginning and ending with noodle mixture. Top with cheese. Bake at 350° for 30 to 35 minutes.

Yield: 6 to 8 servings.

—*Vicki Ballinger*
Stutler, Alberta

If you do not currently make your own ground venison, check out the recipe accompanying the Mexican Lasagna dish on page 165.

DU

Venison Meatloaf

For a hearty family favorite, try this meatloaf. It's also delicious leftover— simply slice it on sandwiches.

2 eggs
1 (8-ounce) can tomato sauce
1 medium onion, finely chopped
1 cup fine, dry breadcrumbs
1½ teaspoon salt
⅛ teaspoon pepper
1½ pounds ground venison
2 tablespoons brown sugar
2 tablespoons spicy brown mustard
2 tablespoons vinegar

Combine first 6 ingredients. Add venison, and mix well. Press into an ungreased 9- x 5-inch loafpan. Combine brown sugar, mustard, and vinegar; pour over meatloaf. Bake at 350° for 1 hour and 10 minutes.

Yield: 6 to 8 servings.

—*Lynn Nyhus*
Sioux Falls, South Dakota

Cajun Meatballs and Spaghetti

½ pound ground lean venison
½ pound ground pork
1 cup fine, dry breadcrumbs
2 eggs
1 teaspoon salt
¼ cup finely chopped onion
2 garlic cloves, finely chopped
2 tablespoons Parmesan cheese
¾ teaspoon ground red pepper
1 (6-ounce) can large button
　mushrooms
1 large onion, finely chopped
2 garlic cloves, finely chopped
1 large bell pepper, finely chopped

3 tablespoons peanut oil
2 (6-ounce) cans tomato paste
2 (15-ounce) cans tomato sauce
½ (10-ounce) can diced tomatoes
　with green chiles
3 cups water
Creole seasoning to taste
2 teaspoons sugar
2 (6-ounce) cans sliced mushrooms
3 tablespoons finely chopped fresh
　parsley
1 (32-ounce) package angel hair
　pasta, cooked

Pasta cools quickly, so toss it as little as possible. Serve this dish with hot garlic bread and a mixed green salad.

Combine first 9 ingredients in a large bowl; roll mixture into 20 balls, placing 1 mushroom in the center of each ball. Place meatballs on a lightly greased baking sheet; bake at 400° for 30 to 40 minutes or until dark brown. Cook onion, garlic, and bell pepper in hot oil 15 minutes or until browned. Add tomato paste and next 4 ingredients, stirring well. Add sugar and meatballs to sauce, and simmer at least 3 hours. Add more water as needed if sauce gets too thick. Add sliced mushrooms and parsley 20 minutes before serving. Serve over pasta.

Yield: 4 to 6 servings.

—Ed Villien
Lafayette, Louisiana

DU

157

Pasta with Venison Sauce
Pasta Sul Cervo: Friuli Style

Add salt to the pasta water only after boiling. Coarse-grain sea salt is preferable to heighten the pasta's flavor. Add 1 teaspoon to every 4 quarts water.

2 medium purple onions, quartered
3 large celery stalks, cut into pieces
3 medium carrots, cut into pieces
3 bay leaves
3 whole cloves
1 garlic clove
2 pounds boneless venison steak
5 cups dry red wine
¼ cup unbleached all-purpose flour
¼ cup olive oil
Coarse-grain sea salt and freshly ground pepper to taste
4 tablespoons tomato paste
3 cups warm chicken broth
1½ pounds wide egg noodles or fettuccine, cooked
10 tablespoons Parmigiana-Reggiano cheese, freshly grated

Combine first 7 ingredients and 3 cups red wine in a shallow glass dish; chill 24 hours, turning twice. Remove meat and vegetables from marinade, discarding marinade. Dredge venison in flour, and sauté in hot oil in a skillet 5 minutes. Chop vegetables, and add to skillet; cook 15 minutes. Add 1 cup wine, and cook 15 more minutes. Add remaining 1 cup wine, and cook 15 minutes. Season with salt and pepper to taste. Combine tomato paste and 1 cup of broth, stirring well. Add mixture to skillet, and simmer 3 hours, adding remaining 2 cups broth as needed and turning meat occasionally. Uncover during last 2 minutes. Pour a small amount of sauce onto a serving platter; add pasta, and top with remaining sauce and cheese.

—*Tom Colligan*
Irvington, Virginia

158

Rotisserie Venison

1 (5- to 7-pound) venison roast
Salt, ground red pepper, and ground
   black pepper to taste
2 garlic bulbs, divided into cloves

24 small red chile peppers
1 onion, chopped
½ gallon buttermilk

Season venison with salt, ground red pepper, and ground black pepper to taste. Cut small slits in venison, and stuff with garlic and chile peppers. Place venison in a large roasting pan, and add onion and buttermilk; chill 1 to 2 days. Remove venison from marinade, discarding marinade. Light barbecue pit, and place coals as far away from meat as possible. Let coals get white. Place venison on a rotisserie, and let pit cool to approximately 400°. Cook venison 2 hours and 30 minutes to 3 hours.

Yield: 6 to 8 servings.

—*Ed Villiex*
Lafayette, Louisiana

Buttermilk reduces the gaminess of venison while the rotisserie keeps this roast moist.

DU

159

Classic Venison Roast

When prepared simply,
venison is naturally low
in fat and cholesterol.
For a tender, delicious
meal, try this classic
recipe.

1 (3- to 5-pound) venison roast
Chopped onion
Garlic cloves
1 cup cider vinegar
Vegetable oil

2 cups strong black coffee
3 cups water
Salt and pepper to taste
Flour

Cut slits in venison, and stuff with onion and garlic. Place roast in a large bowl, and add vinegar, chill 1 to 2 days, turning occasionally. Remove venison from marinade, discarding marinade. Brown in hot oil in a large Dutch oven. Add coffee and 3 cups water. Cover, reduce heat, and simmer 3 hours. Season with salt and pepper to taste 20 minutes before serving. Add flour to pan drippings to make gravy, if desired.

—Dona J. Berge
Dixon, Illinois

Venison Roast Mexicali

1 (4-pound) venison roast
1 cup dry red wine (optional)
1 (1-ounce) envelope dry onion
    soup mix
1 (15-ounce) can pinto beans
1 (15-ounce) can ranch-style beans,
    drained
1 (15-ounce) can kidney beans,
    drained

1 (15-ounce) can chickpeas, drained
1 (15-ounce) can chili with beans
1 (30-ounce) can tamales
1 (10-ounce) can green enchilada
    sauce
Salt and pepper to taste
2 cups (8 ounces) shredded Cheddar
    cheese

Place venison in a large Dutch oven; add wine, if desired, and sprinkle with soup mix. Cover and cook over medium heat 3 to 4 hours or until tender. Shred venison, and place in a large baking dish. Add pinto beans and next 7 ingredients, stirring well. Top with cheese, and bake at 350° for 45 minutes or until bubbly.

Yield: 16 servings.

—*Cheralynn A. Schnepp*
Tucson, Arizona

Most commercially sold venison comes from New Zealand farm-raised deer. Whether bought commercially or harvested by a hunter, deer is most tender when killed between 1 and 2 years of age.

Chinese Style Venison

Keep this delightful meal as healthy as possible. Use light soy sauce, reduced-salt bouillon, and canola or safflower oil.

1 (1½-pound) venison round steak, sliced thinly across the grain
1 cup canola oil
¼ cup soy sauce
¼ teaspoon ground ginger
Pinch of ground red pepper
1 large onion, chopped
2 tablespoons canola oil, for stir frying

6 mushrooms, cut into chunks
1 celery stalk, chopped
1 green bell pepper, cut into strips
½ cup chicken bouillon granules
¼ teaspoon dry mustard
Cornstarch
Hot cooked rice

Combine first 5 ingredients in a shallow dish; cover and chill 3 hours. Stir-fry onion in 2 tablespoons hot oil in a wok over medium-high heat 2 minutes. Push onion to the side; add mushrooms, and stir-fry 2 minutes. Push mushrooms to the side; add celery, and stir-fry 2 minutes. Remove vegetables from wok. Add bell pepper, and stir-fry 1 minute. Remove venison from marinade, reserving marinade. Add venison to wok, and stir-fry 2 minutes. Return vegetables to wok, and add bouillon and dry mustard. Simmer 2 minutes. Add ½ cup reserved marinade, and simmer 2 minutes. Thicken pan drippings with cornstarch and cold water. Serve over buttered rice.

—Donald Smith
Davison, Michigan

Venison Backstrap au Poivre

1 (1-pound) venison tenderloin, cut into 1-inch steaks
Coarsely ground black pepper
4 tablespoons soy sauce

2 to 3 tablespoons butter or margarine
1 cup beef broth
½ cup red wine
Chopped fresh parsley

Press pepper into sides of venison. Combine venison and soy sauce in a shallow dish, and marinate at least 2 hours at room temperature, turning occasionally. Remove venison from marinade, reserving marinade. Melt butter in a skillet; add venison, and sauté 2 to 3 minutes on each side. Remove to a serving platter, and keep warm. Add reserved marinade, beef broth, and wine to pan drippings; bring to a boil, and cook until reduced to 1 cup. Pour over venison. Sprinkle with fresh parsley. Serve with rice and salad.

—Barbara N. Larrabee
Houston, Texas

Parsley is easily grown. No green thumb is needed to grow the herb in small pots. You will be amazed how fresh herbs enhance the flavor of your food.

Bayou Backstrap

This recipe offers a unique way to prepare venison backstrap. The breakfast sausage gives an added dimension to the taste. If Owen's Breakfast Sausage is not available in your area, other brands may be substituted.

1 tablespoon butter or margarine
½ cup diced onion
½ cup diced bell pepper
1 pound Owen's Breakfast Sausage
1 venison tenderloin, butterflied lengthwise and flattened to ¼ inch
Vegetable oil
1 cup water

Melt butter in a skillet; add onion and bell pepper, and sauté until tender. Remove from heat, and add sausage, mixing well. Place stuffing on one-half of venison, and fold to cover. Sew venison edges together using cotton thread. Brown in hot oil in skillet, and place in a roasting pan. Add 1 cup water, and bake, covered, at 350° for 1 hour, adding more water as needed.

—*Manuel David*
Sulphur, Louisiana

Vennie Stew

1 medium-size venison roast, cubed
3 or 4 potatoes, cubed
1 large onion, chopped
1 or 2 carrots, grated or sliced
1 or 2 celery stalks, sliced
½ cup frozen corn, thawed
½ cup frozen peas, thawed

½ green bell pepper, chopped
½ red bell pepper, chopped
½ yellow bell pepper, chopped
1 banana pepper, chopped
¼ cup apple cider vinegar
1 cup cooking wine
Salt and pepper to taste

Combine all ingredients in a large stockpot, and add water to cover. Bring to a boil; cover, reduce heat, and simmer at least 2 hours.

Yield: a whole bunch.

—*James A. "Captain JAG" Gehde*
Lesage, West Virginia

If you're searching for banana peppers in the produce section and you're not sure what they look like, keep their name in mind. Banana peppers are yellow, long, and curved—much like the recognizable fruit.

DU

Grilled Venison Chops

3 tablespoons Worcestershire sauce
3 tablespoons steak sauce
¼ cup olive oil

6 venison chops
1 garlic clove, minced
Freshly ground pepper to taste

Whisk together first 3 ingredients in a small bowl. Brush mixture evenly on venison, reserving remaining marinade. Chill venison 2 hours. Rub venison with garlic, and season with pepper to taste. Grill over medium heat (300° to 350°) 14 minutes, basting with reserved marinade.

—*Gerry Acquilano*
Geneva, New York

If grilling with indirect heat, resist the temptation to lift the grill hood and look at the food. Peeking adds as much as 15 minutes to grilling time.

Venison Pepper Steak

2½ to 3 pounds venison, sliced
    thinly across the grain
1 teaspoon seasoned salt
¼ teaspoon black pepper
2 tablespoons sugar
1 tablespoon vegetable oil
Garlic powder or minced fresh
    garlic to taste

1½ medium onions, diced
2 bell peppers, sliced in strips
2½ tablespoons flour
1 tablespoon beef broth
¼ cup dry white wine
¼ cup vegetable juice
4 ounces fresh sliced mushrooms
    or 1 (4-ounce) can

Cook first 4 ingredients in hot oil in a skillet over high heat until meat is browned. Add garlic powder, onion, and bell pepper, and cook until tender. Add flour, and cook until browned. Add beef broth, wine, and vegetable juice, stirring well. Add mushrooms, and transfer mixture to a slow cooker. Cook on MEDIUM 4 hours or until meat is done.

—Kris Jack
Rhinelander, Wisconsin

For the most flavorful taste, use fresh garlic. Loose bulbs tend to be fresher than boxed garlic. Try using 3 garlic cloves in this recipe.

DU

Autumn Venison Pumpkin Dinner

Pumpkin adds taste, color, and a decorative flair to this meal. The seasonal favorite is a complete meal in itself, yet consider serving it with cornbread.

1 (5- to 8-pound) short pumpkin
1 large onion, chopped
3 garlic cloves, minced
1 tablespoon olive oil
2 pounds ground venison, turkey, or beef
1 (8-ounce) package fresh sliced mushrooms or 2 (4-ounce) cans
1 (8-ounce) can sliced water chestnuts

2 (10¾-ounce) cans cream of mushroom soup, undiluted
3 cups cooked white or brown rice
1 teaspoon Worcestershire sauce
2 teaspoons honey
½ teaspoon ground savory
1 cup water
Salt and pepper to taste

Remove meat from pumpkin, and place in a pan; cover with aluminum foil. Sauté onion and garlic in hot oil until tender; add venison, and cook until meat is browned. Pour off excess grease. Add mushrooms and next 8 ingredients; simmer 5 to 10 minutes. Spoon venison mixture into prepared hollowed-out pumpkin. Cover with pumpkin lid. Bake venison-filled pumpkin and pumpkin meat 1 hour 30 minutes or until pumpkin is tender. Serve venison with a scoop of pumpkin meat.

Yield: 6 to 8 servings.

—*Nancy Malech*
Coyote, California

Venison Medallions with Madeira Cream Sauce

1 pound venison loin steak, cut
  across the grain into ¼-inch slices
1 cup Madeira
3 tablespoons butter or margarine
Ground white pepper to taste

2 tablespoons minced shallots
1 cup sliced mushrooms
3 tablespoons olive oil
3 tablespoons sour cream

Combine venison and Madeira in a shallow dish, and chill 1 hour. Remove venison from marinade, reserving marinade. Melt butter in a skillet; add venison, and cook until browned, sprinkling with pepper after turning. Remove venison from skillet; add shallots and mushrooms, and sauté until browned, adding oil as needed. Add reserved marinade and sour cream to skillet, stirring well. Return venison to skillet, and simmer until thoroughly heated.

Yield: 4 servings.

—*Paul F. Vang*
Butte, Montana

Madeira takes its name from the small island off the Moroccan coast. Different styles of the wine are available, and all generally offer rich, sweet flavors.

DU

Braised Venison Shanks

Although venison shank is somewhat difficult to remove and grind due to numerous tendons, it tenderizes nicely when prepared this way.

4 venison shanks, trimmed
2 garlic cloves, cut into
   10 to 12 slivers each
2 to 3 tablespoons flour
3 tablespoons butter or margarine
1 bay leaf
1 large lemon, grate rind
  and squeeze juice

¼ cup water
Salt and pepper to taste
4 to 6 carrots, cut into thirds
4 medium or 8 small onions, sliced
4 large or 8 to 10 small potatoes,
  peeled and chopped

Cut slits in thickest portions of venison, and stuff with garlic. Dredge venison in flour. Melt butter in a skillet; add venison, and cook until browned. Add bay leaf and next 3 ingredients. Cover, reduce heat, and simmer 2 to 3 hours or until meat is tender, adding water as needed. Add carrot, onion, and potato, and cook until vegetables are done. Remove bay leaf, and discard. Serve with salad and a good red wine.

Yield: 4 servings.

—*Karen and Philip Whitford*
Montello, Wisconsin

174

Grilled Venison with Juniper Berry Sauce

1 pound venison tenderloin, sliced
    across the grain into 1-inch strips
Salt-free herb-and-spice seasoning
Pepper to taste
1 fresh rosemary sprig
1 cup white wine
2 ounces shallots, chopped
1 cup juniper berries or blackberries,
    crushed

2 tablespoons vegetable oil
1 (8-ounce) package mushrooms,
    quartered
4 celery stalks, thinly sliced
1 large rutabaga, thinly sliced
2 parsnips, thinly sliced
Wild rice cooked in veal or
    chicken stock

Juniper berries smell like a fresh pine forest. Always crush the berries before cooking with them in order to release their aroma.

Season venison with salt-free herb-and-spice seasoning, pepper, and rosemary. Combine venison, wine, shallots, and juniper berries in a shallow dish, and chill 1 hour. Remove venison from marinade, reserving marinade. Brown venison in hot oil in a skillet. Add reserved marinade and mushrooms, and bring to a boil. Cook until reduced by half. Remove berries, and add celery, rutabaga, and parsnips; simmer 5 minutes. Remove venison from skillet, and arrange on a bed of wild rice; add sauce and vegetables.

—Tom Colligan
Irvington, Virginia

175

Venison-All-in-One-Dish

Gravy may be prepared by thickening the pan drippings. After removing the meat and vegetables, slowly mix 3 to 4 tablespoons flour with drippings. Bring to a boil; reduce heat, and simmer, stirring constantly, until thickened.

1½ pounds venison chops, trimmed
1 cup white wine
2 tablespoons soy sauce
2 tablespoons lemon juice
1 bay leaf
1 tablespoon garlic salt or 1 garlic
    clove, minced
½ teaspoon ground ginger

3 tablespoons canola oil
¾ cup sliced carrot
⅔ cup sliced mushrooms
½ cup chopped celery
1 beef bouillon cube
Chopped fresh parsley

Combine first 7 ingredients in a shallow dish, and chill 3 to 4 hours. Remove venison from marinade, reserving marinade. Pat venison dry, and brown in hot oil in a skillet. Add reserved marinade, carrot, and next 3 ingredients, adding water if necessary to cover venison. Bring to a boil; reduce heat, and simmer 40 minutes. Remove bay leaf, and discard. Remove venison and vegetables to a serving platter. Sprinkle with parsley before serving.

Yield: 4 servings.

—Randall J. Kelly
Leawood, Kansas

Sauerbraten with Sour Cream Gravy

1 (5-pound) venison roast (top or
    bottom round or rump)
1 tablespoon salt-free herb-and-spice
    seasoning
1 onion, chopped
10 whole peppercorns
3 bay leaves
3 whole cloves
1 cup vinegar
2 cups water
2 ounces salt pork, cut into thin strips

2 tablespoons olive oil
2 tablespoons all-purpose flour
2 tablespoons sugar
7 gingersnaps, crushed (add more
    to thicken gravy)
Salt and pepper to taste
½ cup dry red wine
Sour cream
Hot cooked egg noodles

Rub venison with seasoning, and place in a large bowl. Bring onion and next
5 ingredients to a boil in a large saucepan. Remove from heat, and let cool. Pour
mixture over venison, and add water to cover. Cover and chill 2 days, turning venison
twice each day. Remove venison from marinade, and pour marinade through a
wire-mesh strainer, reserving 4 cups. Cut slits in venison, and stuff with salt pork.
Brown venison in hot oil in saucepan. Remove venison from saucepan, and place in
roasting pan. Add flour to saucepan, and cook until browned. Add reserved
marinade, sugar, gingersnaps, and salt and pepper to taste. Cook until smooth and
creamy; pour over venison. Cover and simmer 2 hours and 30 minutes or until tender,
basting frequently. Add wine during last 30 minutes. Remove venison from pan, and
add sour cream to drippings, stirring well. Serve over egg noodles.

—Jacquie Colligan
Irvington, Virginia

*Sauerbraten is a German
dish using vinegar,
sugar, and seasoning to
marinate pot roast. Do
not omit the gingersnaps
or the flavor will be
incomplete.*

DU

Wild Game Meatloaf

If you cannot find Snappy Tom tomato juice, substitute spicy Bloody Mary mix or vegetable juice.

3½ cups Snappy Tom tomato juice
3 pounds lean ground moose, elk, or venison
1½ cups chopped onion
1½ cups Italian-style breadcrumbs
1 egg
1 (4-ounce) can mushrooms, chopped
3 mild green chiles, chopped
2 to 4 dashes hot sauce
2 to 4 dashes Worcestershire sauce
Pinch of salt
15 shakes Szechuan style pepper blend
3 tablespoons prepared mustard
3 tablespoons brown sugar
3 tablespoons vinegar
1 cup water
2 medium tomatoes, chopped

Combine 2 cups tomato juice and next 10 ingredients, and shape into a loaf. Place in a shallow pan, and bake at 350° for 15 minutes. Combine remaining 1½ cups tomato juice, mustard, and next 3 ingredients, stirring well. Pour over meatloaf. Top with chopped tomato, and bake 1 hour and 30 minutes, basting occasionally.

—Paul Suda
Coeur d'Alene, Idaho

Corned Elk

2 quarts distilled water
½ cup canning and pickling salt
½ cup meat tenderizer
3 tablespoons sugar
2 tablespoons mixed pickling spice
2 bay leaves

Whole black peppercorns
1 or 2 garlic cloves, minced
1 (2- to 3-pound) elk brisket, flank,
    or shoulder roast
Chopped potato
Chopped carrot

Bring first 8 ingredients to a boil in an enamel saucepan. Remove from heat, and cool. Place elk in a large glass bowl, and add brine. Cover with plastic wrap, and chill 4 to 5 days, turning elk occasionally. Drain elk, discarding brine. Rinse with cold water. Place elk in a large Dutch oven, and add water to cover. Bring to a boil; drain. Cover again with cold water. Bring to a boil; cover, reduce heat, and simmer 4 hours or until tender. Add potato and carrot during last 45 minutes.

—*Linda Graham*
Rushville, Nebraska

Feel free to substitute venison for elk in this tender, slow-cooked meal.

Elk Kahlua Kabobs

2 pounds elk, cut into 1-inch strips
Fresh vegetables cut into
   1-inch pieces
¾ cup chicken broth
¾ cup chunky peanut butter

1 ounce Kahlua
1 whole dried red chile pepper
1 garlic clove
¼ teaspoon prepared horseradish

Thread elk and vegetables on skewers. Process broth and next 5 ingredients in a blender until smooth. Brush marinade on kabobs. Grill over medium heat (300° to 350°) until desired degree of doneness, turning and basting with marinade.

—*Elizabeth Rinn*
Jackson, Wyoming

Try bell peppers, onions, cherry tomatoes, or zucchini in this recipe. In order for the meat and vegetables to cook thoroughly, separate items ¼ inch. If you like your meat well done, grill the vegetables on separate skewers .

Wyoming Barbecue

1 elk or moose roast
1 cup of vinegar
¼ cup of ketchup

Buns
Cole slaw
Hot sauce

Cook first 3 ingredients in a slow cooker on LOW 10 hours. Remove elk, and shred. Serve on buns with cole slaw and hot sauce.

—*Elizabeth Rinn*
Jackson, Wyoming

For a hearty sandwich, this slow-cooked meat is sure to hit the spot. The cole slaw cools down the sandwich, so feel free to load on the hot sauce.

DU

Caribou Chili

Venison may be substituted for caribou in this classic chili recipe. For a spicier meal, increase the amount of chili powder or add a dash of hot sauce.

1 pound caribou
1¼ cups minced onion
3 tablespoons vegetable oil
2 (15-ounce) cans kidney beans
1 (6-ounce) can tomato paste

1 (10-ounce) can condensed
  tomato soup
2 tablespoons chili powder
3 tablespoons water
2 teaspoons salt
½ teaspoon pepper

Brown caribou and onion in hot oil in a large skillet. Add kidney beans, tomato paste, and tomato soup, and cook 10 minutes. Combine chili powder and next 3 ingredients, stirring to make a paste. Add chili mixture to skillet, and simmer 45 minutes, stirring frequently. Serve immediately.

—*George S. Brown*
Oshkosh, Wisconsin

Antelope-Garden Vegetable Linguini

1 pound antelope sausage
5 green or red bell peppers,
  cut into strips
1 (3-ounce) can chopped black olives
1 small bag frozen peas, thawed

4 to 5 large carrots, sliced
2 cups linguini, cooked
1 cup Italian dressing
Garlic powder
Dried oregano

Cook first 5 ingredients in a saucepan over medium heat until sausage is browned. Combine sausage mixture, pasta, and next 3 ingredients in a large bowl, tossing to coat. Serve hot or cold

—Elizabeth Rinn
Jackson, Wyoming

If you don't make your own sausage, commercially prepared sausage, such as Italian, may be substituted.

Antelope Steak

4 antelope steaks, tenderized
2 eggs, lightly beaten

4 cups crushed saltine crackers
Salt and pepper to taste

Dip antelope in egg, and dredge in cracker crumbs. Brown antelope in a lightly greased ovenproof skillet. Season with salt and pepper to taste. Bake at 375° for 1 hour, turning at least once.

—*Betty Hrdlicka*
Dorchester, Nebraska

This cooking method reduces the gamey taste of the meat. Keep in mind that wild game continues to cook after removing it from heat. Be careful not to over-cook it.

Wisconsinized Moose Chili

2½ pounds boneless moose or
   venison, cut into ½-inch cubes
2 tablespoons vegetable oil
2 cans Wisconsin beer (1 goes in
   the chili, 1 goes in the cook)
¾ cup water
1 (16-ounce) can diced tomatoes
2 (8-ounce) cans tomato sauce
1 (4.5-ounce) can chopped
   green chiles
1 green bell pepper, chopped
1 medium onion, chopped

1 garlic clove, chopped
4 teaspoons chili powder
⅛ teaspoon cayenne pepper
½ teaspoon ground black pepper
½ teaspoon ground white pepper
½ teaspoon dried crushed oregano
1 teaspoon ground cumin
1 teaspoon salt
1 cup (4 ounces) shredded
   Monterey Jack cheese
Toppings: chopped onions, sour
   cream, tortilla chips

Brown elk in hot oil in a large saucepan; drain, and add 1 can beer, ¾ cup water, and next 13 ingredients. Bring to a boil; reduce heat, and simmer 3 hours, stirring occasionally and adding more water as needed. Add cheese during last 20 minutes. Serve with desired toppings and more beer.

—Donald Gantner
Random Lake, Wisconsin

This wild game chili recipe is designed for tame taste. If you appreciate the burn of a good chile pepper, increase the amount of chili powder, cayenne, and white pepper.

Moose Stroganoff

2 pounds cubed moose (or venison, elk, or beef)
1 large onion cut into large pieces
2 cups fresh sliced mushrooms
2 (10¾-ounce) cans cream of mushroom soup, undiluted

1 (10¾-ounce) can cream of celery soup, undiluted
¼ teaspoon black pepper
Salt to taste

Combine all ingredients in roasting pan. Bake, covered, at 400° for 45 minutes. Reduce heat to 225°, and bake 2 more hours. Serve over pasta or mashed potatoes.

Yield: 6 servings.

—Sheila Vigenski
Bad Axe, Michigan

To judge how much pasta to cook, calculate 4 ounces per person. For exceptionally hungry hunters, consider boosting that quantity to 6 ounces.

Bubble and Squeak

Butter or margarine
2 pounds moose or deer round steak
1 (4-ounce) can mushrooms
2 cups cubed white potato
4 cups sliced onion
½ cup hot water

1 (10¾-ounce) can cream of chicken
    soup, undiluted
1½ tablespoons brown sugar
1 cup cold water
2 teaspoons salt
½ teaspoon pepper
1 can French fried onions

Melt butter in a large skillet; add moose, and cook until browned. Transfer moose to a 2-quart baking dish. Drain mushrooms, reserving liquid; add mushrooms, potato, and onion to baking dish. Combine reserved mushroom liquid, ½ cup hot water, and next 5 ingredients in a saucepan, stirring well. Cook until bubbly. Add sauce to baking dish. Top with fried onions, and bake, covered, at 350° for 2 hours. Uncover and bake 1 more hour.

Yield: 6 to 8 servings.

—*Wayne L. Ballinger*
Endiang, Alberta

Although well known in Canada, this meat-and-vegetable dish differs widely from house to house. The origin of this meal may come from England, where cabbage is used as an ingredient in this vocal dish.

DU

Boris and Natasha's Secret Chili

If moose and squirrel are out of your reach, try other meat combinations such as 1 pound ground venison and ½ pound Italian sausage. No matter what combination you choose, you will find this to be a full-bodied, savory chili.

2 medium-size yellow onions, coarsely chopped
½ cup olive oil
1 pound ground moose (Bullwinkle)
½ pound squirrel, cubed (Rocky)
1 teaspoon olive oil
2 (12-ounce) bottles amber ale
1 (28-ounce) can plum tomatoes with juice
3 to 4 tablespoons chili powder

1 teaspoon ground cumin
1 tablespoon dried oregano
½ teaspoon ground ginger
½ teaspoon salt
¼ teaspoon ground allspice
1 cup water
2 (14-ounce) cans kidney beans
2 (15-ounce) cans black beans, rinsed and drained
6 garlic cloves, minced

Sauté onion in ½ cup hot oil in a large Dutch oven over medium heat until tender. Brown moose and squirrel in 1 teaspoon hot oil in a skillet 8 to 10 minutes. Drain excess fat. Add moose and squirrel to onion, and reduce heat. Add beer and tomatoes, stirring tomatoes with spoon to break up. Add chili powder and next 6 ingredients; cover, if desired, and simmer 1 hour. Add beans and garlic; cover and simmer at least 30 minutes, stirring occasionally.

Yield: enough for 4 to 6 hungry spies.

—Joe Quinn
Calgary, Alberta

Barbecued Bear

¼ cup vinegar
2 tablespoons sugar
½ teaspoon pepper
¼ teaspoon garlic powder
1 onion, minced
1 teaspoon chili powder
5 drops hot sauce
½ cup water

1 teaspoon dry mustard
1½ teaspoons salt
1 tablespoon lemon juice
¼ cup vegetable oil
½ cup ketchup
2 tablespoons Worcestershire sauce
1 bear roast

Combine first 12 ingredients in a saucepan; simmer 20 minutes. Add ketchup and Worcestershire sauce, and bring to a boil. Remove from heat. Bake bear at 325° for 3 to 4 hours or until tender, basting frequently with sauce.

—*JoAnn MacRaild*
Wooster, Ohio

Getting the bear is the hard part, cooking and enjoying it is easy. While the meat roasts, sit back and tell the tales of your hunt.

Grilled Leg of Goat

1 hindquarter of young goat, trimmed
1 garlic clove
1 teaspoon salt
¼ teaspoon pepper

1 cup vinegar
¼ teaspoon ground cumin
½ teaspoon dried crushed rosemary

You can also bake the goat at 350° for 1 hour and 30 minutes. Don't forget to baste the meat with the drippings.

Rub goat with garlic, salt, and pepper. Combine vinegar, cumin, and rosemary in a small bowl. Grill goat over high heat (400° to 450°) 1 hour and 30 minutes or until no longer pink, basting with vinegar mixture and turning every 15 minutes.

Yield: 8 to 10 servings.

—Helene Gross
Kalamazoo, Michigan

Wild Boar Supreme

Flour
Salt and pepper to taste
6 wild boar chops or
    1 (2- to 3-pound) boar roast
¼ cup olive oil
1 (8-ounce) package fresh
    sliced mushrooms
1 onion, thinly sliced
1 (10¾-ounce) can cream of
    mushroom soup, undiluted

½ cup sour cream
½ cup whipping cream or
    half-and-half
½ cup apple juice or white wine
½ teaspoon crushed rosemary
¼ cup brandy
1 can French fried onions
Hot cooked noodles

Combine flour and salt and pepper to taste; dredge boar in flour mixture. Brown boar in hot oil in a skillet. Drain boar on paper towels, and place in a lightly greased 13- x 9-inch baking dish. Add mushrooms and onion to skillet, and sauté until tender. Add soup and next 4 ingredients, stirring well. Pour mushroom mixture over boar. Bake, covered, at 350° for 1 hour. Uncover, and add brandy. Sprinkle with fried onions, and bake 10 more minutes. Serve over buttered noodles.

—*Nancy Malech*
Coyote, California

To make ahead of time, prepare up to the point of topping with the fried onions. Cool the baked boar, and chill up to 24 hours.

Squirrel Casserole

2 squirrels, cooked and deboned
2 (10-ounce) packages frozen
   broccoli with cheese
1 stick butter or margarine
1 cup chopped onion

1 cup chopped celery
1 (10¾-ounce) can cream of
   mushroom soup, undiluted
1 cup cooked rice

Bring squirrel and water to cover to a boil in a saucepan; boil until meat is tender and falls from bones. Cook broccoli according to package directions, and drain. Melt butter in a skillet; add onion and celery, and sauté until tender. Add soup to skillet, stirring well. Combine squirrel, broccoli mixture, and rice in a 13- x 9-inch baking dish. Bake at 350° for 1 hour. Serve with Vienna bread, applesauce, or salad.

Yield: 2 servings.

—*Mr. and Mrs. Isaac Kirk, Sr.*
Silver Spring, Maryland

Whatever your meat source, this versatile casserole tastes great. Try it with beaver, snapping turtle, squirrel, or venison. Remember to cut the meat small and debone it.

Baked Squirrel with Cream Sauce

1 cup flour
1 teaspoon seasoned salt
½ teaspoon pepper
3 to 4 pounds squirrel, cut into pieces
¼ cup butter or margarine
1½ cups water

3 teaspoons chicken bouillon
  granules
2 tablespoons minced onion
½ cup white wine
½ cup sour cream

Combine first 3 ingredients in a shallow dish. Dredge squirrel in flour mixture. Melt half the butter in a skillet; add squirrel, and cook until browned, adding butter as needed. Add 1½ cups water, bouillon, and onion to skillet; reduce heat, cover, and simmer 30 minutes or until squirrel is tender. Remove squirrel to a warm platter, and keep warm. Add wine and sour cream to skillet, and cook 2 minutes. Serve sauce over squirrel.

Yield: at least 4 servings.

—*Darrell Hallau*
Covington, Kentucky

Wild game is naturally low in fat and cholesterol. To make this baked dish even healthier, use nonfat sour cream and light margarine.

Oven Barbecue Rabbit

Rabbit meat is tender, flavorful, and naturally low-fat. Try substituting it for chicken in other recipes. For this dish, you may also use squirrel.

2 rabbits
½ cup flour
½ cup vinegar
1½ cups water

1 tablespoon dried crushed
   red pepper
1 stick butter or margarine
1 teaspoon salt

Bring rabbit and water to cover to a boil in a saucepan; boil until rabbit is almost fork-tender. Drain rabbit, and rinse. Dredge rabbit in flour, reserving remaining flour; place rabbit in a Dutch oven. Add remaining flour, vinegar, and remaining ingredients. Bake, covered, at 350° for 45 minutes. Increase heat to 400°; uncover and bake 30 minutes, basting frequently with drippings. Remove rabbit to a serving platter, and bring pan drippings to a boil; cook until reduced by one-third. Serve sauce over rabbit.

—J. Hancock
Gallatin, Tennessee

194

Rabbit with Rosemary

2 tablespoons butter or margarine
1 rabbit, cut into pieces
2 tablespoons flour
2 tablespoons olive oil
Salt and pepper to taste

½ teaspoon dried rosemary
½ teaspoon dried oregano
Dried sage
1 cup beef bouillon granules

Melt butter in a skillet; add rabbit and next 3 ingredients, and cook until rabbit is browned. Transfer rabbit mixture to a 1-quart baking dish, and add rosemary and remaining ingredients, stirring well. Bake, covered, at 400° for 40 minutes. Drain off liquid, and bake, uncovered, 10 more minutes.

—*Elaine French*
Greensboro, North Carolina

If available, use fresh rosemary and oregano. Substitute 2 tablespoons fresh herbs for ½ teaspoon dried.

DU

Rabbit with Mustard

Dry mustard is often used in English cooking. Thanks to Mrs. Clements of Durham, England, mustard seed began to be milled and found its way into culinary history.

1 tablespoon flour
1 tablespoon dry mustard
1 rabbit, jointed
2 tablespoons vegetable oil
6 tablespoons butter or margarine
1 onion, sliced
⅔ cup light ale or cider
1¼ cups chicken stock

Salt and pepper to taste
1 tablespoon vinegar
1 tablespoon Demerara sugar
1 tablespoon Dijon mustard
¼ cup fresh breadcrumbs
2 tablespoons vegetable oil
1 teaspoon chopped fresh chives
1 tablespoon chopped fresh parsley

Combine flour and dry mustard; dredge rabbit in flour mixture, reserving remaining flour mixture. Brown rabbit in hot oil in a skillet; transfer rabbit to a 2-quart baking dish. Melt 2 tablespoons butter in skillet; add onion, and sauté until tender. Add remaining flour mixture, and cook 1 minute. Gradually add ale and chicken stock, and bring to a boil. Season with salt and pepper to taste, and add vinegar, sugar, and Dijon mustard, stirring well. Pour onion mixture over rabbit. Bake, covered, at 350° for 1 hour or until tender. Melt remaining 4 tablespoons butter in skillet; add breadcrumbs and oil, and cook until golden brown, stirring often. Add chives and parsley, stirring well. Sprinkle rabbit mixture with breadcrumb mixture, and serve immediately.

—*Peter Pramphorn*
Leicester, England

196

Grilled Rabbit

1 tablespoon gin
2 teaspoons vegetable oil
1 teaspoon lemon juice
1 teaspoon chopped onion

4 dried juniper berries, crushed
½ teaspoon grated lemon rind
⅛ teaspoon pepper
1 rabbit, cut into pieces

Combine all ingredients in a large bowl, stirring to coat. Cover and chill 2 hours or overnight, turning occasionally. Remove rabbit from marinade, reserving marinade. Grill over medium-high heat (350° to 400°) 30 minutes or until rabbit is tender, turning occasionally and basting with marinade.

—*Betty L. Smolinski*
Appleton, Wisconsin

Because marinades enhance the delicate flavor of rabbit, grilling is the perfect method for cooking it. To add to the pine flavor brought on by the gin and juniper berries, sprinkle pine nuts over the rabbit before serving.

Barbecue Rattlesnake

This whimsical recipe tastes great, so alcohol is actually optional. Mesquite chips work well if oak bark is not available.

1 3-foot long, 2-inch round rattlesnake, skinned and cut into 4-inch pieces

1 bottle Italian dressing
1 to 2 pounds oak tree bark

Marinate snake 4 to 8 hours in dressing. Build a fire using oak tree bark. Barbecue over medium-high flames until golden brown. Serve several drinks before offering to your guests.

—Bob Henke
Richland, Washington

Turtle Cacciatore

¼ cup olive oil
2 ounces salt pork, diced
4 tablespoons butter or margarine
3 pounds turtle meat, cut
   into bite-size pieces
½ pound chicken livers, chopped
½ teaspoon garlic salt
1 teaspoon dried rosemary

1 teaspoon chopped fresh parsley
½ teaspoon freshly ground
   black pepper
½ teaspoon salt
4 tomatoes, chopped
1 tablespoon tomato paste
Hot cooked spaghetti (optional)

Cook first 3 ingredients in a large saucepan until thoroughly heated. Add turtle and chicken livers, and cook 10 minutes or until browned. Add garlic salt and next 6 ingredients, and simmer 30 minutes or until turtle is tender. Serve over pasta, if desired.

—*Eric Debus*
Bella Vista, Arizona

Cacciatore refers to a hunter, in Italian. Just about anything a hunter brings home will work well in this recipe. If using meat more delicate than turtle, omit salt pork and chicken liver. To round out the taste, add green bell peppers.

Frog Legs

This French classic can be made at home with freshly gigged frogs. For a European taste, add 1 garlic clove, minced, with the scallions.

3 tablespoons vegetable oil
½ teaspoon finely chopped scallions
1 teaspoon vinegar
Salt and pepper to taste

6 pairs frogs legs
Flour
1 tablespoon bacon fat
2 tablespoons butter or margarine

Combine first 4 ingredients; dip frog legs in mixture, and dredge in flour. Fry frog legs in bacon fat and butter until browned. Serve as for fried chicken. This is enough for two or three servings. The taste of frog legs is a cross between fish and chicken.

Yield: 2 to 3 servings.

—*Ralph L. Givens*
Cedaredge, Colorado

SEAFOOD

Of course, nothing tastes better than seafood that goes straight from the water to the skillet or stockpot, but even a stint in the freezer won't diminish the flavors these recipes will enhance. Since the experts agree that fish is an important part of a healthy diet, you'll be glad to provide these nourishing dishes to your family.

—*Billy Joe Cross*

Spicy Italian Catfish

Instead of the fish, use 6 to 8 skinless boneless chicken pieces. After simmering 20 minutes, keep covered and cook 1 hour. Uncover and cook 40 more minutes.

2 cups water
1 can diced tomatoes
1 (10-ounce) can diced tomatoes
  with green chiles
1 (8-ounce) can tomato sauce
1 tablespoon minced garlic
Salt and pepper to taste

1 teaspoon dried basil
1 teaspoon dried oregano
2 (4-ounce) cans sliced mushrooms
1 to 2 pounds skinless boneless
  catfish pieces
Hot cooked pasta

Bring first 9 ingredients to a boil in a large saucepan. Add catfish, and bring back to a boil. Cover, reduce heat, and simmer 20 minutes. Uncover, and cook 15 more minutes or until thickened. Serve over pasta.

—*J. Steven Blount*
Lake Charles, Louisiana

Salmon with Vinegar-Honey Glaze

2 tablespoons balsamic vinegar
2 tablespoons honey
1 tablespoon coarse-grained
  Dijon mustard

½ teaspoon minced garlic
4 large salmon fillets, with skin
Salt and pepper to taste

Combine first 4 ingredients, and brush generously on salmon; season with salt and pepper to taste. Place salmon in an aluminum foil-lined pan, and bake at 450° for 5 minutes per inch of thickness.

—*Maria T. Boone*
La Plata, Maryland

Balsamic vinegar has been made in Italy for nearly 1,000 years. It was so coveted that families considered the vinegar an heirloom and handed it down in their daughters' dowry.

DU

203

Stuffed Fish

You'll want to make extra stuffing with this delicious meal. Bake the additional stuffing, covered, in a buttered baking dish.

1 salmon, trout, or bass
Salt and pepper to taste
1 small onion
1 (8-ounce) package sliced
    fresh mushrooms
Vegetable oil
2 cups soft breadcrumbs

½ cup milk
1½ to 2 cups grated carrot
1½ tablespoons dried parsley flakes
4 tablespoons butter or margarine,
    melted
2 tablespoons lemon juice
Garlic powder to taste

Rub salmon cavity with salt and pepper to taste. Sauté onion and mushrooms in hot oil in a skillet until tender. Combine onion, mushrooms, breadcrumbs, and next 3 ingredients in a bowl, stirring well. Spoon stuffing into salmon cavity; close cavity with skewers or string. Combine butter, lemon juice, and garlic powder to taste in a small bowl, stirring well. Brush fish with butter mixture, and place in a shallow pan. Bake fish at 350° for 1 hour or until fish flakes easily with a fork, basting with butter mixture occasionally.

—*Mitchell Hoy*
Rockwell, Iowa

Shiitake Fillets

4 tablespoons butter or margarine
1 onion, finely chopped
1 teaspoon chopped shallots
1 garlic clove, minced
2 tablespoons tarragon wine vinegar

¼ teaspoon dried thyme
1 handful shiitake mushrooms,
  chopped
1 pound walleye or catfish fillets
Garnish: large shiitake mushrooms

Melt butter in a skillet; add onion and next 5 ingredients, and sauté 5 minutes. Place walleye on top of onion mixture; cover and cook over low heat 10 minutes. Remove walleye from skillet, and place on a heated platter; keep warm. Bring onion mixture to a boil; boil until reduced by half. Pour sauce over walleye, and serve. Garnish, if desired.

—Todd McMullin
Stone Mountain, Georgia

You can substitute morels or portobello mushrooms for shiitake mushrooms, if desired. But avoid using mellow mushrooms, such as button or white.

205

Walleye au Gratin

With its tender flesh, walleye is a perfect fish for pan-frying. Serve this dish with rice or quartered new potatoes that have been buttered and browned.

1 pound walleye fillets
Salt and pepper to taste
2 tablespoons vegetable oil
Juice of 1 lemon
2 tablespoons butter or margarine
1 small onion, chopped
1 (10-ounce) package frozen spinach, thawed, drained, and chopped
$\frac{1}{4}$ teaspoon ground nutmeg
2 small tomatoes, thinly sliced
$\frac{1}{2}$ cup (2 ounces) shredded mozzarella

Season walleye with salt and pepper to taste. Sauté walleye in hot oil in a skillet; add lemon juice, and cook 2 minutes on each side. Remove walleye from skillet, and set aside. Melt butter in skillet, and add onion and spinach. Season with salt and pepper to taste, and add nutmeg. Sauté 2 minutes, and remove from heat. Spread spinach mixture in the bottom of a baking dish, and top with walleye. Place tomato on top of walleye, and sprinkle with cheese. Bake at 375° for 6 minutes or until cheese melts and fish is done. Serve immediately.

—Joe Harvey
Indianapolis, Indiana

Washington State Poor Man's Lobster

1 teaspoon salt
1 tablespoon Old Bay
    Seafood Seasoning
2 cups water

¼ cup cider vinegar
1 pound walleye fillets, cubed
Melted butter

Bring first 4 ingredients to a boil in a saucepan. Add fish. Cover and cook 10 minutes. Drain and serve with melted butter.

—Bob Henke
Richland, Washington

Due to the cost and unavailability of fresh lobster, many of us are faced with finding substitutes for the savory seafood. This recipe is so good that you might opt for the white-fleshed fish over the elite crustacean just for the outstanding taste.

DU

Foil Fish

Fish fillets
Lemon pepper
Lawry's seasoning

2 to 3 tablespoons butter or
 margarine per fillet
Sliced onion

Place each fillet in the center of a large piece of aluminum foil. Season with lemon pepper and Lawry's seasoning. Top with butter and onion. Bring ends of foil up to center of fillet, and fold over twice to make a seam leaving enough foil for expansion. Fold end seams to seal. Bake at 350° for 15 minutes or until foil expands.

—*Carol Olson*
Fairmont, Minnesota

This dish will soon become a family favorite. It's quick, easy, and leaves no dirty dishes. You can also grill the fish packages over medium heat (300° to 350°) for 15 minutes.

Golden Fish Cakes

1 pound cooked whitefish, cod, or
   haddock
1½ cups soft breadcrumbs
3 eggs
2 to 4 tablespoons water
1 medium onion, chopped
2 tablespoons mayonnaise

1½ teaspoons dry mustard
1 teaspoon dried parsley flakes
¾ teaspoon salt
1½ cups Italian-seasoned
   breadcrumbs
2 tablespoons vegetable oil
Tartar sauce (optional)
Lemon (optional)

Combine first 9 ingredients in a large bowl, mixing well. Shape mixture into 12 patties, adding water if needed; coat with Italian-seasoned breadcrumbs. Cook fish cakes in hot oil in a large skillet 4 to 5 minutes on each side or until brown. Serve with tartar sauce and lemon, if desired.

—Glenn Mehring
Carrington, North Dakota

Make sure you use dry mustard, not prepared mustard. The dry version is said to be an "invention" of Mrs. Clements of Durham, England. She made quite a tidy profit selling the milled mustard seeds to patrons including King George I.

DU

Big Walleye Eating at Its Best

Walleye fillets
2 eggs
½ cup favorite beer (optional)

Saltine cracker crumbs
Olive oil

This recipe can be adapted for most fish fillets. To enhance flavor, skin or fillet fresh fish prior to freezing for storage.

Cut walleye into small pieces. Combine eggs and, if desired, beer; dip walleye in mixture, and dredge in cracker crumbs. Allow to set for 2 to 4 minutes on waxed paper. Fry walleye in a small amount of hot oil in an electric skillet at 350° until golden brown. Drain on paper towels.

—*Gary A. Ruggiero*
Fremont, Ohio

Scott's Beer Batter Fish

1 cup flour
1 teaspoon baking powder
2 teaspoons paprika
1 egg

1 cup beer
Salt and pepper to taste
Fish fillets
Vegetable oil

Combine first 6 ingredients in a bowl, stirring well. Dip fish fillets in beer batter. Cook fish in hot oil in a large skillet until golden brown.

—*Scott H. Leininger*
Olathe, Kansas

Cooking fillets in a skillet with oil no more than ¼-inch deep is preferred. If fat intake and cholesterol are not concerns, go ahead and deep-fry it.

211

Belanger Bay Bass

You should be able to smell the potent Greek seasonings when cooking this fish. The result will be a dish that smells as good as it tastes.

6 (1-pound) or 3 (2-pound) bass
Egg
Milk
5 to 6 cups fine, dry breadcrumbs or
    saltine cracker crumbs
2 to 3 tablespoons Greek seasoning

¼ teaspoon garlic salt
½ teaspoon lemon pepper
½ cup chopped fresh parsley
Vegetable oil
Fresh lemon juice

Fillet bass; skin and remove lateral line. Cut each side into 3 pieces, and cut shoulder piece. Combine egg and milk in a shallow dish. Combine breadcrumbs and next 4 ingredients in a zip-top plastic bag. Dip bass in egg mixture, and place in zip-top plastic bag, shaking to coat. Pour oil to a depth of ¼ inch in a large skillet. Heat to 375°; add fish, and fry 2 minutes on each side or until golden brown.

—Kim Black
Aylmer, Ontario

Uncle Ernie's Broiled Garlic Fish Fillets

2½ to 3 pounds catfish fillets
Salt and pepper to taste
⅓ cup olive oil
4 to 6 garlic cloves, minced
Juice of 1 large lemon

Pinch of dried thyme
Pinch of dried oregano
Lemon wedges
Hot cooked rice

Season catfish with salt and pepper to taste. Whisk together oil and next 4 ingredients in a small bowl. Place catfish in a lightly greased shallow roasting pan; add oil mixture. Broil 20 minutes. Serve with lemon wedges and rice.

Yield: 4 servings.

—*Claudia F. Williams*
San Antonio, Texas

When buying garlic, look for bulbs that are hard, not shrunken. Upon opening garlic, cut away any odd-colored portions. This part may leave a bad taste and spoil the dish.

DU

Salmon Soufflé

4 eggs, separated
2 tablespoons butter or margarine
2 tablespoons flour
1 cup milk
⅛ teaspoon salt

Dash of cayenne pepper
Dash of hot sauce
Dash of Johnny Seafood seasoning
1 pint salmon

Combine egg yolks, butter, and next 6 ingredients in the top of a double boiler; bring water to a boil. Reduce heat to low; cook, stirring often, several minutes. Beat egg whites in a small bowl until stiff. Add salmon to double boiler, and fold in egg whites. Pour mixture into a baking dish, and bake at 325° for 1 hour and 20 minutes. Serve immediately.

Yield: 4 servings.

—*Sanna G. Levan*
Seward, Alaska

To fold in egg whites, lay a scoop of stiff eggs on the fish mixture using a spatula. With the spatula, gently incorporate the fish mixture into the eggs. Continue this folding motion until the food is mixed.

214

Swordfish with Fennel Seeds

1 garlic clove, cut in half
1 pound swordfish steaks
1 teaspoon plus ½ cup dry vermouth
2 teaspoons olive oil

1 teaspoon dried rosemary
1 teaspoon fennel seeds
1 tablespoon butter or margarine

Rub garlic on both sides of swordfish, and sprinkle with 1 teaspoon vermouth, oil, rosemary, and fennel seeds. Place swordfish in a shallow dish; cover and chill 2 hours. Scrape the rosemary and fennel seeds off the swordfish, and discard; broil swordfish 6 inches from heat 4 to 6 minutes on each side. Transfer swordfish to a warm serving platter. Cook remaining ½ cup vermouth in a small saucepan over high heat until reduced to 3 tablespoons. Add butter to saucepan, stirring well. Pour sauce over swordfish.

Yield: 2 servings.

—*Bob Ette*
Guntersville, Alabama

The Canadian Fisheries rule of thumb for cooking fish is to cook 10 minutes per inch of thickness. Make sure you measure the fish at its thickest point.

DU

Swordfish Destiny

Swordfish steaks
Dale's Steak seasoning

Lawry's Lemon Pepper
Parmesan cheese

If you don't have much time for preparation, this recipe is perfect. Generally, fish only take about 15 to 30 minutes to marinate. That's much quicker than the average meat and poultry marinating time.

Marinate fish in Dale's Steak seasoning 30 minutes. Remove swordfish from marinade, discarding marinade; pat dry with a paper towel. Sprinkle swordfish with lemon pepper, and grill, covered with grill lid, over medium heat (300° to 350°) 10 minutes on each side. Sprinkle with Parmesan cheese, and close grill lid. Cook just until cheese melts and fish flakes easily with a fork.

—Robert Joyner
Flovilla, Georgia

Grouper with Almond Sauce

¼ cup white wine
½ cup apple cider vinegar
2 tablespoons fresh lemon juice
¼ cup prepared mustard
1 tablespoon dried dillweed

Pepper to taste
Chopped garlic cloves
2 pounds Grouper
½ cup almonds, coarsely crushed
Lemon rind, sliced into 1-inch pieces

Combine first 7 ingredients in a shallow dish, stirring well. Add grouper, turning to coat; chill 1 to 2 hours. Remove grouper from marinade, reserving marinade. Grill grouper over medium heat (300° to 350°) 5 minutes on each side or until fish flakes easily with a fork, basting with reserved marinade. Top each piece of grouper with crushed almonds and a piece of lemon rind.

Yield: 4 servings.

—*Ralph D. Jones*
Johnson City, Tennessee

1 pound almonds in their shell = 1 cup whole almond meat = 1½ cups chopped almonds; 4 ounces shelled almonds = 1 cup almonds

Pan Fried Scallion Fillets

For the best flavor, do not omit the chopped cilantro. It adds a fresh, sharp taste to the crisp, delicious fillets. Place the fillets on a serving platter, and garnish each fillet with three scallions. Sprinkle with the chopped cilantro.

½ cup olive oil
18 scallions, white bulb and 5 inches green
1 teaspoon coarsely ground black pepper
1 teaspoon dried thyme leaves
1 tablespoon chopped fresh parsley
1 cup milk

1 cup yellow cornmeal
1 cup unbleached all-purpose flour
½ teaspoon cayenne pepper
Salt and freshly ground black pepper, to taste
6 fresh fillets (2 to 2½ pounds total)
1 cup unsalted butter, clarified
1 tablespoon chopped cilantro

Heat the olive oil in a large skillet over medium heat. Add the scallions, and cook, turning them with tongs, until just wilted, 2 minutes. Sprinkle with pepper and thyme as they cook. Remove the scallions from the skillet, sprinkle them with the parsley, and set aside. Pour the milk into a glass pie plate. Mix the cornmeal, flour, cayenne, and salt and pepper together in a second pie plate. Dip the fillets first in the milk, then in the cornmeal mixture. Melt the butter in a large skillet over medium heat. Sauté the fish until golden on both sides, 3 minutes per side.

—Charlie Jolley
Spokane, Washington

Honey Barbecue Halibut Steaks

Honey
Olive oil

Teriyaki sauce
1 (8-ounce) halibut steak per person

Combine equal amounts of honey, oil, and teriyaki sauce in a bowl, stirring well; add halibut, and chill 30 minutes. Grill halibut over medium heat (300° to 350°) 5 minutes on each side or until fish flakes easily with a fork.

—*Bob Gibson*
Cottonwood, California

Although commercial barbecue sauces are offered in a variety of flavors, this honey grilling sauce is easy to prepare and delicious.

Grilled Bluefish Fillets

Bluefish fillets, with skin　　**Old Bay seasoning**
Lemon juice　　**Salt and pepper to taste**
Mayonnaise

Bluefish often has a strong taste, but the flavorful ingredients of this recipe eliminate much of this "fishy" flavor.

Place bluefish, skin side down, on aluminum foil, and sprinkle with lemon juice. Spread mayonnaise over bluefish, and sprinkle with Old Bay seasoning and salt and pepper to taste. Seal foil over top of bluefish. Grill over high heat (400° to 450°) 12 to 15 minutes or until fish flakes easily with a fork.

—Bob Meyers
Wind Gap, Pennsylvania

Spicy Pepper Grilled Fish

1 to 1½-inch-thick amberjack,
   red snapper, or ling fillets
Italian dressing (do not use fat-free)
1 purple onion, sliced
Juice of 1 lime
Jalapeño, serrano, or habañero
   peppers, sliced

Cayenne pepper
Paprika
Ground black pepper
Ground white pepper
Lemon pepper
Pinch of ground turmeric

Combine all ingredients in a shallow dish, stirring to coat; chill 30 minutes to 4 hours. Remove amberjack from marinade, reserving marinade. Grill amberjack over high heat (400° to 450°) until each side is seared. Pour reserved marinade into a shallow pan made from aluminum foil. Add fish, and place pan on grill. Grill over high heat until fish flakes easily with a fork.

—*Carl Degner*
Pasadena, Texas

Serve this spicy fish on a bed of rice with a liberal spoonful of sauce, onions, and peppers. An excellent addition is crusty bread for sopping up the sauce.

DU

Grilled Speckled Trout

5 pounds speckled trout fillets, with skin
Ground red pepper
Garlic powder
Salt and ground black pepper to taste

White wine vinegar
Worcestershire sauce
Garnishes: chopped green onions and chopped fresh parsley

To check fish for doneness, remove from the grill, and gently separate the flesh at its thickest point using a sharp knife. If the center of the flesh appears opaque, your fish is done. Fish that appears predominately transparent should be returned to the fire.

Season trout with red pepper, garlic powder, and salt and black pepper to taste; place in a shallow dish, and add vinegar and Worcestershire sauce. Chill overnight. Preheat barbecue pit until coals are white hot. Make sure the coals are at least 12 inches from the grilling screen. Grill trout, skin side down, on a greased grilling screen over direct heat 15 to 20 minutes or until fish flakes easily with a fork. Remove the skin before serving. Garnish, if desired.

Yield: 4 to 6 servings.

—*Ed Villien*
Lafayette, Louisiana

222

Blackened Catfish

1 (8-ounce) catfish fillet　　　　**¼ cup Cajun Spice**
2 tablespoons olive oil

Brush catfish with oil, and dredge in Cajun Spice. Cook catfish in a skillet over medium-high heat until blackened on the outside but flaky and moist within, turning once.

Yield: 1 serving.

Cajun Spice

¼ cup garlic powder　　　　**2 tablespoons dried basil**
¼ cup onion powder　　　　**2 tablespoons dried thyme**
¼ cup ground cumin　　　　**2 tablespoons dried oregano**
¼ cup paprika　　　　　　　**2 tablespoons black pepper**
¼ cup chili powder　　　　　**1 teaspoon cayenne pepper**
3 tablespoons Old Bay seasoning

Combine all ingredients in a bowl, stirring well. Store in an airtight container.

—*H. Craig Carson*
Clinton, Oklahoma

The perfect accompaniment to this dish is red beans and rice. You might want to add a pinch of Cajun Spice, which is used on the fish, in your beans and rice.

DU

223

Stir-fried Shrimp and Vegetables

Chinese cabbage is also called bok choy. It is a mild-flavored vegetable that appears as a cylindrical bundle of leaves. You can find it in the produce section of most supermarkets.

3 tablespoons water
1 tablespoon cornstarch
1 tablespoon reduced-sodium
  soy sauce
1 teaspoon sugar
1 small head Chinese cabbage,
  coarsely chopped
1 bunch green onions, sliced
  diagonally into ¼-inch pieces

2 tablespoons vegetable oil
1 pound unpeeled, medium-size
  fresh shrimp
¼ teaspoon ground ginger
½ teaspoon dried red pepper flakes
1 (15-ounce) can straw mushrooms
Cashews (optional)
Hot cooked brown rice

Combine first 4 ingredients in a small bowl. Stir-fry cabbage and green onions in hot oil in a wok 2 minutes. Add 1 tablespoon cornstarch mixture, and cook 1 minute. Remove cabbage mixture from skillet, and place on a serving platter; keep warm. Peel shrimp, and devein, if desired. Stir-fry shrimp, ginger, and red pepper in skillet 2 minutes, adding more oil if needed. Add mushrooms and remaining cornstarch mixture. Cook 2 minutes, and spoon over vegetables on serving dish. Top with cashews, if desired. Serve over brown rice.

Yield: 4 servings.

—*Dianne Mortimer*
Newport, Oregon

Tiger Shrimp or Fish

**2 pounds peeled, large fresh shrimp
   with tails, or 2 pounds fish fillets**
1 cup water
Juice of 3 lemons

1 stick butter or margarine, melted
1 bottle Tiger Sauce
1½ cups chopped green onions
Creole seasoning

Place shrimp in a single layer in a 13- x 9-inch baking dish. Add 1 cup water and next 3 ingredients. Sprinkle with green onions and Creole seasoning. Bake at 350° for 35 to 40 minutes. When this dish is done, the remaining liquid is known as "Tiger Juice" and is delicious when spooned onto a baked potato or soaked up with French bread.

—*Kim Burton*
Marshall, Texas

This spicy recipe can be used with either shrimp or fish fillets such as catfish, crappie, or red snapper. Thicker fish fillets may need to bake an additional 10 minutes.

DU

Shrimp-and-Cheese Casserole

1 pound unpeeled, medium-size fresh shrimp
6 bread slices, torn into small pieces
2 cups (8 ounces) grated Old English cheese
4 tablespoons butter or margarine, melted

3 eggs
½ teaspoon dry mustard
Salt and pepper to taste
2 cups milk
1 garlic clove (optional)

Peel shrimp, and devein, if desired. Place half of shrimp in the bottom of an 8-inch square baking dish; add half each of bread and cheese. Repeat layers with remaining shrimp, bread, and cheese. Top with melted butter. Combine eggs, next 3 ingredients, and, if desired, garlic, stirring well; pour over mixture in baking dish. Cover and chill 3 hours or overnight. Bake, covered, at 350° for 1 hour.

Yield: 4 servings.

—*Julie Skierkowski*
Memphis, Tennessee

Broiled Shrimp and Crab

6 ounces Garlic Butter
18 medium-size fresh shrimp, peeled
and deveined

1 pound jumbo lump crabmeat

Melt 2 ounces Garlic Butter in a skillet; add shrimp, and sauté until done. Place half the crabmeat in an ovenproof baking dish; add shrimp, and top with remaining half of crabmeat. Spread remaining 4 ounces Garlic Butter over crabmeat. Cover and bake at 400° for 10 minutes. Uncover during last 2 minutes.

Garlic Butter

6 ounces butter or margarine,
softened
½ teaspoon garlic powder

½ teaspoon MSG
1 teaspoon chopped fresh parsley
1 ounce white wine

Blend first 4 ingredients in an electric blender at a low speed 13 minutes. Gradually add wine, and mix 10 more minutes.

—*Richard Tonelli*
Crisfield, Maryland

Shrimp is sized

as follows:

Jumbo: 10 per pound

Large: 10 to 25 per pound

Medium: 25 to 40 per
pound

Small: 40 to 60 per pound

Tiny: More than 60 per
pound

Crab Cake Batch

In crabmeat, lump refers to the grade of meat. Often called jumbo lump, or backfin, this white meat is chunky and of excellent quality.

2 teaspoons butter or margarine
½ cup diced celery
¼ cup diced onion
¼ cup diced green onions
¼ cup diced mushrooms
½ teaspoon minced garlic
1½ teaspoons Dijon mustard
2 teaspoons chopped fresh parsley
1 teaspoon lemon juice
1½ teaspoons Worcestershire sauce
2 tablespoons white wine

½ teaspoon chopped fresh dill
½ teaspoon Hungarian paprika
¼ teaspoon cayenne pepper
Salt and pepper to taste
2 egg yolks, lightly beaten
¾ cup soft breadcrumbs
1 cup lump crabmeat, drained
Vegetable oil
Marinara Sauce
Garnish: lemon wedges

Melt butter in a large skillet; add celery and next 4 ingredients, and sauté until tender. Remove from heat, and add mustard and next 8 ingredients, stirring well. Add egg yolks and breadcrumbs to mixture, stirring well. Fold in crabmeat, and chill 30 minutes. Shape crab mixture into small patties, and fry in a small amount of hot oil in a skillet until lightly browned, turning once. Serve hot with Marinara Sauce. Garnish, if desired.

Yield: 2½ cups.

—*Murphy Baytta*
Philadelphia, Pennsylvania

Easy Crab Cakes

½ pound crabmeat, broken up
½ pound imitation crabmeat,
  broken up
2 tablespoons mayonnaise
1 teaspoon finely chopped green
  bell pepper
1 teaspoon dried parsley flakes
1 teaspoon prepared mustard

1 teaspoon seafood seasoning
  (optional)
¼ teaspoon salt
¼ teaspoon pepper
1 egg, beaten
3 slices white bread with crusts,
  crumbled
Butter or margarine for browning

In a large bowl, combine first 11 ingredients. Mix well and form into 6 or 8 patties. Melt butter in a large frying pan and cook patties over medium-high heat until browned on both sides.

Yield: 3 to 4 servings

—*Michael Copper*
Daytona Beach, Florida

Here's an inexpensive and easy way to make crab cakes. To reduce costs even more, try using poached fish. White-fleshed fish, such as walleye or even cod, work great. You might want to mix in a little crab to maintain the traditional taste.

DU

Seafood Gumbo Kaplan-style

½ pound unpeeled, medium-size
    fresh shrimp
¼ pound crabmeat
1 (8-ounce) container oysters
1 large onion, diced
3 garlic cloves, minced
2 to 3 tablespoons dark roux

½ cup dry white wine
8 cups water or seafood stock
Salt and pepper to taste
Hot sauce
¼ pound bay scallops, sliced
Hot cooked white rice

To store live shellfish, wrap in paper towels, and chill on a dish. Never store shellfish in water or ice because they naturally open and close their shells.

Peel shrimp, and devein, if desired. Drain crabmeat, and flake, removing any bits of shell. Drain oysters, reserving juice. Combine oyster juice, onion, and next 6 ingredients in a large stockpot. Heat almost to boiling; reduce heat, and simmer 2 hours. Add seafood, and simmer 5 more minutes. Turn off heat, and let stand 10 minutes. Serve over white rice.

—*Steve Comeaux*
Hot Springs, Arkansas

Oysters á la Ritz

5 tablespoons plus 1 teaspoon butter
    or margarine, softened
1 tablespoon minced fresh parsley
2 garlic cloves, minced
Juice of 2 limes
4 tablespoons brandy
16 fresh oysters (preferably belon)

8 ounces cooked lobster or crabmeat
2 medium tomatoes, peeled, seeded,
    and diced
5 tablespoons plus 1 teaspoon
    ketchup
6 tablespoons grated Parmesan
    cheese

Combine first 3 ingredients in a small bowl, stirring to make a paste. Combine lime juice and brandy in a separate bowl. Shuck oysters, and add oyster meat to lime mixture. Discard the top shell, and rinse the bottom shell of sand and debris. Layer 1 teaspoon butter mixture, 1 oyster, ½ ounce lobster, a bit of diced tomato, and 1 teaspoon ketchup in each oyster shell. Flatten mound slightly using the back of a spoon, and sprinkle ½ tablespoon Parmesan cheese over each. Place oysters on a rack in a broiler pan. Broil 3 to 4 minutes or until cheese is lightly browned.

Yield: 4 servings.

—*Theador Fuzie*
Montreal, Quebec

In England, ketchup was made with vinegar and either mushrooms or oysters. Tomatoes weren't added to this popular condiment until later in the 18th century when American settlers moved West.

DU

231

Vongole Ripieni Puccini (Baked Clams)

Common Clams:

- **Hard-shell (quahog)**
  Use: small ones eaten
  raw; large ones used
  in chowder

- **Soft-shell (steamer)**
  Use: steamed or fried

- **Razor**
  Use: steamed

- **Geoduck**
  Use: sliced, fried, or
  chopped up for
  chowder

12 clams, scrubbed and cleaned
1 teaspoon chopped garlic
3 teaspoons olive oil
3 teaspoons fine, dry breadcrumbs
1 teaspoon chopped fresh parsley
4 teaspoons chopped crabmeat
½ teaspoon dried oregano
⅛ teaspoon cayenne pepper
Salt to taste
2 tablespoons dry white wine

Steam clams in a small amount of water until shells open. Cut clamshells apart at hinges, and remove clams. Drain well, and set shells aside. Process clams in a food processor 5 to 10 seconds. Do not puree. Sauté garlic in 1 teaspoon hot oil in a small skillet until lightly browned. Remove from heat, and add breadcrumbs and next 5 ingredients, stirring well. Place clamshells on a baking sheet, and top evenly with chopped clams. Sprinkle evenly with breadcrumb mixture, and drizzle with remaining 2 teaspoons olive oil. Bake at 350° for 12 to 15 minutes or until lightly browned. Remove from oven, and sprinkle with wine.

Yield: 4 servings

—*José Voltair*
San Diego, California

Clam Fettuccini

1 cup butter or margarine
½ cup olive oil
4 garlic cloves, minced
½ cup chopped white onion
2 green onions, thinly sliced
1 cup whipping cream
1 small can milk or
   1 cup half-and-half
1 cup white wine
½ teaspoon ground savory

1 teaspoon dried parsley flakes or
   1 tablespoon chopped fresh parsley
3 cups finely chopped tomato
1 pound fresh clams, chopped, or 2 to
   3 cans chopped clams, undrained
Salt and pepper to taste
Juice of half a lemon
2 (8-ounce) packages fresh or
   16-ounces dried fettuccini, cooked
Freshly grated Parmesan cheese

Melt butter in a skillet; add oil, garlic, and onions, and sauté until tender. Add whipping cream and next 4 ingredients. Bring to a high simmer (do not boil); cook 6 minutes or until liquid is reduced by one-fourth. Add tomato, and cook over medium heat 2 minutes. Add clams, and cook 5 minutes or until clams are done. Season with salt and pepper to taste, and add lemon juice. Serve sauce over pasta. Top with Parmesan cheese.

Yield: 6 to 8 servings.

—*Nancy Malech*
Coyote, California

Cook pasta in plenty of boiling water. As a general rule, use 4 quarts water per 1 pound pasta. Large amounts of water take quite a while to reach a rapid boil, so plan ahead.

DU

Teriyaki Scallops with Asparagus

Japanese cuisine often calls for mirin, which is a sweet cooking wine. For this recipe, avoid mirin with labels marked "flavored" or "seasoned." Look for the basic wine called hon-mirin, manjo-mirin, sweet cooking sake, or sweet cooking rice wine.

2 tablespoon soy sauce
1 tablespoon mirin
2 teaspoons sake
1 teaspoon sugar
1 pound large scallops (trimmed, if desired)

8 ounces asparagus
2½ cups water
¼ teaspoon salt
1 tablespoon vegetable oil

Mix first four ingredients in medium bowl; stir to dissolve sugar. Add scallops; let stand 10 minutes, turning occasionally. Drain scallops, reserving marinade. Cut asparagus spears crosswise into halves. Heat water and salt to boiling in 2-quart saucepan over high heat; add asparagus. Reduce heat to medium-high; boil gently until crisp-tender, 3 to 5 minutes. Drain; keep warm. Heat broiler; brush broiler rack with oil. Place scallops on rack; brush lightly with marinade. Broil about 4 inches from heat source until brown, 4 to 5 minutes. Turn scallops; brush lightly with marinade. Broil just until scallops are opaque in center and cooked through, 4 to 5 minutes. Serve immediately with asparagus; pass pan juices from skillet or remaining marinade, if desired.

Yield: 4 servings

—*Kathleen Johnson*
Carmel, California

DESSERTS AND DRINKS

If you have any room left for dessert after enjoying any of the delicacies prescribed in this book, here are some great ideas for the *pièce de résistance* of your meal. All you need is a recliner and some quiet time, and you'll think heaven has arrived at your home.

—*Billy Joe Cross*

Wild Turkey Bourbon Brownies

When a plain brownie just won't do, try this spiked version of the classic.

1 package brownie mix
⅓ cup Wild Turkey bourbon
1 stick butter or margarine, softened
3 tablespoons Wild Turkey bourbon

1 pound powdered sugar
2 tablespoons butter or margarine
1 cup (6 ounces) semisweet chocolate morsels, melted

Prepare brownies according to package directions. Cool and pour ⅓ cup bourbon over top. Combine 1 stick butter, 3 tablespoons bourbon, and powdered sugar, stirring until smooth. Spread over brownies. Combine butter and melted chocolate, stirring until smooth. Spread over frosted brownies. Chill 30 minutes.

—*James L. Nelson*
Valparaiso, Indiana

Awesome Cherry Crisp

2 (20-ounce) cans cherry pie filling
½ cup flour
2 cups uncooked regular oats
2 cups brown sugar
½ teaspoon salt

1 teaspoon cinnamon
½ teaspoon nutmeg
6 tablespoons butter or margarine,
   softened

Pour cherry pie filling in a shallow 28- x 18-inch baking dish. Combine flour and next 5 ingredients in a large bowl. Add butter, stirring well. Spread topping evenly over pie filling. Bake at 375° for 30 minutes.

—*Scott H. Leininger*
Olathe, Kansas

Almost any type of canned fruit filling may be substituted for cherry. Avoid seedy fruits, such as black- berries, because they may add unwanted texture.

DU

237

Heavenly Dessert

Here's an easy recipe that is out-of-this-world delightful. Angel food cake is already fat free, so to further reduce fat and calories, use sugar-free pudding and fat-free frozen whipped topping.

1 (3.4-ounce) package vanilla instant pudding mix
1 commercial angel food cake, torn into pieces
1 pint strawberries, sliced
1 to 2 bananas, sliced
2 kiwi, sliced
1 pint blueberries or raspberries
1 (8-ounce) container frozen whipped topping, thawed
Assorted fruit for decoration (optional)

Prepare pudding according to package directions. Layer half each of angel food cake pieces, pudding, fruit, and whipped topping in a medium bowl. Repeat procedure with remaining ingredients. Add fruit on top for decoration, if desired.

—Beth Hays
Gulfport, Mississippi

238

Harvest Pie

1 (15-ounce) package refrigerated
   piecrusts
4 medium Granny Smith apples,
   peeled and sliced
1 cup cranberries
½ cup golden raisins
½ cup chopped walnuts

1 cup sugar
⅔ cup brown sugar
4 tablespoons flour
1 teaspoon cinnamon
¼ teaspoon nutmeg
3 tablespoons butter or margarine,
   cut up

Fit 1 piecrust into the bottom of a 9-inch pieplate according to package directions. Combine apple slices and next 9 ingredients in a large bowl, stirring well. Pour into pieplate, and dot with butter. Top with remaining piecrust, sealing with a fork. Bake at 400° for 45 minutes.

—Susan M. Berger
Thousand Oaks, California

After a feast of wild game, round out the meal with this bountiful offering. Walnuts add the perfect woody taste to this pie. Pecans may be substituted, if desired.

DU

239

Daiquiri Pie

To decrease chilling time, place the bowl of filling mixture in a larger bowl of ice and water. Stir until the mixture is cold.

1½ cups light rum
1 (4 serving size) package lemon instant pudding and pie filling
1 (3 oz.) package lime flavored gelatin
⅓ cup sugar
2½ cups water

2 eggs, slightly beaten
2 cups non dairy whipped topping, thawed
1 (9-inch) crumb crust, baked and cooled

Mix pudding, gelatin and sugar in saucepan. Stir in ½ cup water and eggs; blend well. Add remaining water. Stir over medium heat until mixture comes to full boil. Remove from heat; stir in rum. Chill about 1½ hours. Blend topping into chilled mixture. Spoon into crust. Chill until firm, about 2 hours. Garnish with additional whipped topping and lime rings.

—Pete Jensen
South Bend, Indiana

Classic Carrot Cake

2 cups sugar
1½ cups vegetable oil
4 eggs, lightly beaten
2 cups all-purpose flour
2 teaspoons baking soda
1 teaspoon salt
2 teaspoons ground cinnamon
1 teaspoon grated nutmeg
¼ teaspoon ground allspice

3 cups finely shredded carrot
  (6 to 8 carrots)
½ cup chopped walnuts
½ cup unsalted butter, softened
1 (8-ounce) package cream cheese,
  softened
2 cups powdered sugar
2 teaspoons vanilla extract

Beat first 3 ingredients in an electric mixer until blended. Combine flour and next 5 ingredients in a separate bowl. Gradually add dry ingredients to the sugar mixture, blending well after each addition. Gently fold in carrot and walnuts. Pour mixture into a buttered 13- x 9-inch baking dish. Bake at 325° for 1 hour to 1 hour and 10 minutes or until a wooden pick inserted in the center comes out clean. Remove to a wire rack to cool. Beat butter in an electric mixer until light and fluffy. Work cream cheese into butter using a fork. Add powdered sugar and vanilla, and beat vigorously, until blended. Spread cake with frosting.

Yield: 12 servings.

—Sue Chapel
Palm Beach, Florida

Doctors say you should eat plenty of vegetables, but this cake satisfies your sweet tooth, not your daily recommended amount of carotene.

Potato Chip Cookies

½ cup butter, softened
½ cup margarine
½ cup sugar
1½ cups all-purpose flour

1 teaspoon vanilla
¾ cup crushed potato chips
Powdered sugar

Beat first 3 ingredients at medium speed with an electric mixer until light and fluffy. Add flour and vanilla, stirring well. Gently fold in potato chips. Drop by teaspoonfuls onto ungreased baking sheets. Bake at 350° for 12 to 15 minutes or until edges are lightly browned. Cool on wire racks, and dust with powdered sugar.

Yield: 4 dozen.

—*Clair Bryan*
Cordova, Tennessee

If you do a lot of baking, set aside small amounts of morsels, nuts or candy pieces and soon you will have enough mix to take on the trail. If you know you'll be hiking in the heat, substitute candy-coated chocolate for morsels to prevent the snack mix from melting.

Triple-Chocolate Cookies

6 (1-ounce) squares semisweet
   chocolate, coarsely chopped
2 (1-ounce) squares bittersweet
   chocolate, coarsely chopped
6 tablespoons unsalted butter
⅓ cup all-purpose flour
1 teaspoon baking powder
¼ teaspoon salt

2 eggs
1 tablespoon powdered instant
   espresso coffee
2 teaspoons vanilla extract
¾ cup sugar
2 cups chopped walnuts
6 (1-ounce) squares milk chocolate,
   chopped

Combine first 3 ingredients in the top of a double boiler; bring water to a boil. Reduce heat to low; cook, stirring often, until chocolate melts. Set aside to cool. Combine flour, baking powder, and salt in a small bowl. Beat eggs, espresso, and vanilla at low speed with an electric mixer. Increase speed to high, and gradually add sugar, beating until light and fluffy. Add melted chocolate mixture to egg mixture, beating at low speed until well blended. Gradually add flour mixture, beating at low speed. Add walnuts and milk chocolate, stirring well. Drop dough by rounded tablespoonfuls 2 inches apart on lightly greased baking sheets. Bake at 325° for 15 to 20 minutes. Cool on wire racks.

Yield: 2 dozen.

—Marie Wienckowski
Aurora, Illinois

Here's a cookie chock full of great flavor. For a delicate change, substitute 1 cup chopped pecans and 1 cup crushed macadamia nuts for walnuts.

DU

Chocolate Lovers Snack Mix

2 cups milk chocolate morsels
2 cups white chocolate morsels
2 cups chocolate covered raisins

2 cups white or dark chocolate
  covered pretzels
1 cup chocolate covered peanuts
1 cup cashew halves

Combine all ingredients; store in airtight container or zip-top bag.

Yield: 10 cups.

Crisp and light, these cookies are delicious. No one imagines that potato chips are an ingredient unless you tell them.

Skinny Snack Mix

3 cups low fat granola cereal
2 cups reduced fat honey roasted
  peanuts

2 cups reduced fat chocolate morsels
1 cups golden raisins

Combine all ingredients; store in airtight container or zip-top bag.

Yield: 10 cups.

—*Woody Rutland*
Birmingham, Alabama

Georgia Peach Melba

1 (10-ounce) package frozen
   raspberries, thawed
1½ tablespoons sugar
3 tablespoons raspberry liqueur

1 (16-ounce) can sliced peaches, well
   drained, or 4 fresh pitted peaches
2 pints French vanilla ice cream

Puree raspberries and sugar in a food processor. Add liqueur. Use sauce immediately, or chill. Place a peach half, cut side up, in each individual serving dish. Top with 1 scoop vanilla ice cream and raspberry sauce. Serve immediately.

Yield: 8 servings.

—*Sue Olbman*
Atlanta, Georgia

In Puerto Rico, law requires rum to age in oak barrels for no less than one year. Aging and filtration creates a smooth spirit perfect for enhancing punches or mixes.

DU

245

Hot Cherry Pie

1 fifth amaretto
1 quart cranberry juice
½ pint vodka (optional)

Combine amaretto, cranberry juice, and, if desired, vodka in a coffeepot; heat.

Here's a collection of beverages sure to be the hit of the party.

Watermelon Punch

2 quarts fresh orange juice
2 quarts pineapple juice
1 fifth Southern Comfort
1 fifth almond liqueur
Garnish: pineapple and orange slices

Combine first 4 ingredients in a large punch bowl, stirring well. Garnish, if desired.

—Tom Colligan
Irvington, Virginia

Big Red Punch

2 (46-ounce) cans red punch
1 (6-ounce) can frozen orange juice
   concentrate, undiluted
1 (6-ounce) can frozen lemonade
   juice concentrate, undiluted

1 (750ml) Bacardi light rum
Garnish: slices of strawberries,
   oranges, lemons, and limes

Combine all 4 ingredients. Chill 2 hours. Pour punch over block of ice in punch bowl. Float garnishes on top. Serve in 6 ounce punch cups.

Yield: 22 servings

—M.J. Belfour
Boston, Massachusetts

Peach Melba takes its name from the lovely opera performer Nellie Melba. She rode atop a stage swan and inspired the scrumptious dessert. Add a swan base to your creation if you want to be true to form.

DU

Brandy Alexander

4 ounces brandy
4 ounces white creme de cocoa

1½ pints vanilla ice cream
Garnish: nutmeg and 4 whole filberts

A delectable afterdinner drink or late evening repast. Consume with caution—too many of these will sneak up on the unwary imbiber, even when leisurely sipped.

Combine first three ingredients in blender and whip until mixture achieves a thick, smooth texture. Pour into tulip glasses and sprinkle with nutmeg. Float a single filbert on surface.

Yield: 4 servings

—*Mary Petrie*
Superior, Wisconsin

Cool-La, Jamaican Coffee Liqueur

4 cups sugar
½ cup instant coffee granules
1½ cups water

1 fifth vodka
1 vanilla bean, split, or vanilla
flavoring (do not use extract)

Cook first 3 ingredients in a saucepan until dissolved. Remove from heat, and cool. Pour into a ½-gallon container, and add vodka and vanilla bean. Chill at least 2 weeks.

—Terry Hamlett
Charlottesville, Virginia

Although nothing beats authentic Kahlua, this recipe offers a satisfying alternative. Serve either half-and-half or milk with this drink, if desired.

Alcohol-free Cajun Mary

When alcohol is not on your list of desired ingredients, enjoy this spicy concoction. Don't forget to garnish it with a short stalk of celery.

1 cup vegetable juice or no-salt-added
   vegetable juice
1 teaspoon taco sauce
½ teaspoon prepared horseradish
½ teaspoon ground cumin
¼ teaspoon chili powder
Dash of hot sauce

Combine all ingredients in a small pitcher. Serve in a 10-ounce glass over ice.

Yield: 1 cup.

—*Rob Rash*
Marion, Arkansas

Frozen Watermelon Slushy

2 cups water
¾ cup sugar
1 (12-ounce) can frozen fruit punch
   concentrate, thawed
5 cups cubed and seeded watermelon

1 tablespoon lemon juice
1 (1-liter) bottle lemon-lime soft
   drink, chilled
2 ounces vodka (optional)
Garnish: watermelon wedges

Bring water and sugar to a boil in a saucepan, stirring until sugar dissolves. Boil 3 minutes. Remove from heat. Add punch concentrate, stirring until dissolved. Process 2½ cups watermelon and lemon juice in a food processor until smooth. Add to punch mixture. Process remaining 2½ cups watermelon, and add to punch mixture. Place in a plastic container, and cover. Freeze at least 8 hours or until firm. To serve, scrape the frozen mixture with a spoon to form a slush. Spoon 1 cup slush into a 12-ounce tumbler. Slowly add ½ cup soft drink per serving. Garnish, if desired.

Yield: 8 servings.

—D. William Ziske
Vancouver, British Columbia

Make a batch ahead of time, and store it in the freezer. It will keep frozen for weeks. Watermelon slushies look as good as they taste. Beauty drink, eh?

DU

251

Lemon Smoothy

4 cups lemon sherbet
1 cup frozen lemonade concentrate,
  thawed

1 teaspoon lemon juice
3 cups warm water
Garnish: lemon slices

If you are tired of plain, old lemonade, shake it up and have a smoothy. You might even try a shot of rum in it.

Beat first 4 ingredients at low speed with an electric mixer 5 minutes or until smooth. Chill. Serve in tall glasses over ice, and garnish, if desired.

Yield: 1 quart.

—*Diane Harvey*
Wallace, Michigan

252

Fisherman's Delight

Cracked ice
1 ounce vodka
½ ounce clear orange liqueur
¼ cup orange juice

¼ cup cranberry juice
¼ cup sour mix
½ ounce cherry brandy
Garnishes: orange slices and cherries

Fill 1 (8-ounce) glass with cracked ice. Add vodka and next 4 ingredients, stirring lightly. Float cherry brandy on top. Garnish, if desired.

Yield: 1 serving.

—*Joe Starbuck*
Golden, Colorado

Whether you fish or not, this drink is a delight. The sweet berry flavors are the perfect contrast to the tangy citrus flavors. You don't need to be around open water to enjoy this beverage.

Hollandaise Coffee

1 ounce cognac
1 ounce chocolate-mint liqueur
Coffee
Whipped cream
Garnish: fresh mint leaves

Combine cognac and liqueur in a footed mug. Add coffee to fill, and top with whipped cream. Garnish, if desired. Serve immediately.

Yield: 1 serving.

Coffee drinks are a great way to wind down after a wonderful meal.

Almond Coffee

1¼ ounces almond liqueur
¾ ounce brandy
Coffee
Whipped cream
Garnish: maraschino cherry

Combine almond liqueur and brandy in a footed mug dipped in sugar. Add coffee to fill. Top with whipped cream. Garnish, if desired. Serve immediately.

Yield: 1 serving.

—*Tom Jensen*
Chicago, Illinois

Index

Index

Index

Index

Index

Index

Index

Index

ORDERING INFORMATION

Mail to:
Ducks Unlimited, Inc.
One Waterfowl Way
Memphis, TN 38120

Wild Feasts

DUCKS UNLIMITED GAME AND FISH COOKBOOK

Include:

NAME _____

ADDRESS _____ APT. _____

CITY _____ STATE _____ ZIP _____

PHONE _____

QUANTITY	X	PRICE	=	AMOUNT
_____		$24.50 ($32 *CANADA*)		$ _____
To order *Wild Feasts*, **make checks payable to Ducks Unlimited**	PLUS SHIPPING & HANDLING $4 First copy to address above		=	$ _____
	ADDITIONAL COPIES @ $3 Mailed to the same address		=	$ _____
	TOTAL AMOUNT		=	$ _____

Additional copies of *Wild Feasts, A Ducks Unlimited Game and Fish Cookbook* may be ordered from Ducks Unlimited, Inc., One Waterfowl Way, Memphis, TN 38120, at $24.50 (*$32 Canada*) per copy plus $4 shipping and handling for the first copy, plus $3 shipping and handling for each additional copy. Please make checks payable to Ducks Unlimited.

VISA or MasterCard telephone orders may be placed by calling 1-800-45-DUCKS. Please allow three to four weeks delivery unless express delivery is required. Special handling available upon request.

Also consult Ducks Unlimited about these waterfowl-related titles:

161 Waterfowling Secrets

Autumn Passages

Dabblers & Divers: A Duck Hunter's Book

Natural History of the Waterfowl

Book ordering 1-800-45-DUCKS